This book is dedicated to the family

Captain William Henry Hughes, DSC.

Master Mariner

Captain William Henry Hughes, DSC

Dewi B. Francis

Master Mariner— Captain William Henry Hughes, DSC
first published in Wales by
BRIDGE BOOKS
61 Park Avenue
Wrexham
LL12 7AW

© 2006 Dewi B. Francis
© 2006 Design and typesetting, Bridge Books

ISBN 1-84494-030-6

A CIP entry for this book is available from the British Library

Cover illustration:
Scotia *entering Holyhead Harbour, 1930*
© Brian Entwistle

Printed and bound by
Cromwell Press
Trowbridge

Contents

Introduction

This story begins in the 1840s when a young tailor named Lewis Hughes arrived in the small town of Tremadoc and set up a tailor and draper's shop. Some later members of the family believe that he came from either Arklow or Wexford in Ireland, but, although it is quite possible that he learnt his trade in one, or both, of these Irish towns, the census of 1881 clearly gives his place of birth as the village Llanystumdwy, in about 1823.

Tremadoc was a new town, built by William Alexander Madocks, MP, on the expected route of the new road between London and Dublin. Madocks had already reclaimed over 2,000 acres of land from the sea, using his own money and a method he had seen employed on the Thames estuary near his brother's home. Within two years, he was growing oats, wheat, barley and grass on fields that had previously been under the sea. For this feat the Board of Agriculture awarded him its Gold Medal. He had also successfully introduced a Bill to Parliament to make Porthdinllaen the harbour for the Irish Sea traffic, which was expected to increase dramatically following the 1801 Act of Union with Ireland.

The town of Tremadoc itself was a model of town planning. Ideally situated, it had all the conveniences for the weary traveller *en route* to or from Ireland. Hundreds of people had come to see this show town, many of whom had stayed to work, or to start their own trade or business. Such a man was Lewis Hughes. Unfortunately for Madocks and his plans, Porthdinllaen was not chosen as the port for Ireland, losing out to Holyhead by a single vote, and the expected travellers never came. To this day the roads leading from the town's square are called London Road and Dublin Street. Lewis Hughes' tailoring shop was located on London Road.

Maenofferen Quay, Porthmadog with stacked slates awaiting shipment. The brig Excelsior *is berthed on the right. [GAS XS/ 2129/85e]*

Undaunted, Madocks immediately set to work on a new venture. He decided to re-direct the river Glaslyn, and build an embankment, strong enough to carry a road and a railway from the quarries of Ffestiniog to a proper dock, and thus connecting the counties of Caernarfonshire and Meirionethshire. There was already a small fishing port there called Pen Tywyn but it was far too small for what Madocks envisaged. He wanted a proper, deep-water harbour with quays where slates from the various quarries could be stacked. His right-hand man in all this was a young man named John Williams from the Brynsiencyn area of Anglesey who, having gone to Tremadoc to look for a labourer's job, was spotted by Madocks as a potential manager, and promoted. He eventually took over the development entirely when Madocks became too ill to continue.

The job of building the harbour was given to Griffith Griffiths and his four sons. They completed the huge task ahead of time, mainly because the diverted river Glaslyn itself had dredged a great deal of the soil, leaving an ideal deep harbour. Apart from the original wharf, which was soon inadequate for the number of quarry owners who demanded quick access and exit, there soon appeared other wharves, which the quarry owners built themselves, grudgingly paying Madocks for the privilege. In no time, there were ships in the harbour taking slates from Maenofferen, Oakley, Llechwedd and the other quarries in the area to all parts of the world.

The previous method of exporting slate had been by horse-drawn carts or horse-drawn rail to the *Traeth Bach* on the Dwyryd estuary. There they transferred to flat-bottomed boats or barges, which took their loads to the small ships that anchored as near as possible to the shore. This was tedious and dangerous on a calm day, but as the prevailing estuary winds were south-westerly, there was always great difficulty and danger, particularly in rough weather. The slates were heavy and needed careful handling. There was a group of men clad in heavy clothes, wearing breeches and tall hats called 'Philistines', who monopolised this job. Nobody knew much about their background, but everybody seemed to have kept clear of them as far as possible.

Proper packing or protection of the fragile slate was difficult and even the smallest crack or broken corner meant a total loss. Even more care was required in stacking on board ship, using straw and strips of wood called 'laths' or 'ribs'. The mate was always in charge of stacking.

The next stage was to build the new town around the harbour which became known as Porthmadog. Madocks had proved his ability to plan a town in Tremadoc, this project had to be much bigger because of the demand and the urgency for homes, with the resultant need for shops and services. Nor could anyone stop the demand for ships to move the slates, which were the cause of the prosperity. This was really a 'boom town' and, under boom town conditions, corners were cut. Certain areas, such as the High Street (then named Holborn Street, after the street where Madocks had been born in London) and Cornhill, were up to his standards with wide streets and excellent buildings, but then the pressure of demand caused a relaxation and, as in all boom towns, inferior standards were accepted.

Madocks suffered from ill health, due no doubt to his non-stop activities, and his wife took him on the Grand Tour to Italy. They were in Paris on the return journey when he died and he was buried there. He had not lived to enjoy the success of his new town; nor did he witness the lowering of standards in the planning and construction of the new town, which would have deeply offended him.

Porthmadog became well known throughout the world and the languages of many countries could be heard in the small port. Local men travelled widely, not only taking slates, but also fetching goods of all kinds — timber from Scandinavia, beans from north Africa and so on. A regular run for some ships was Porthmadog to Cadiz for salt, then on to Labrador and Newfoundland to deliver the salt to several small ports and creeks where they were loaded with fish which was delivered to Malaga or Genoa or any of the Mediterranean ports. If there were no cargo for the return journey, rather than pay for ballast, they would buy coal or any commodity that would re-sell in Porthmadog.

Lewis Hughes had wisely moved his shop from Tremadoc to 130 High Street, Porthmadog — a wide street with attractive frontages. As everybody needed clothes, Lewis Hughes was mentioned in the *Gazetteer* as one of nine tailors and drapers in the town. He catered for all requirements, from uniforms to overalls, warm weather clothes as well as Arctic wear. As a result, he became quite wealthy. He had married Mary, a lady from nearby Penmorfa, and they had five children, namely; Jane, Robert, Hugh, Harry and Elin.

In order to invest his money, Lewis bought several properties in Porthmadog and Borth-y-gest. He had noticed, however, that some of his best customers had interests, or shares, in ships. These shares were sold in 64ths of the value of the ship. What was, perhaps, of more interest to him was the fact that these shareholders were also, because of their shareholdings, able to get jobs on the various vessels for their sons. His three boys had no interest whatsoever in becoming tailors or drapers, and spent their time near the docks, listening to tales of foreign lands and the escapades retold, and no doubt embellished, by their older friends. These tales fired their desire to go to sea. Bob, the eldest son, had already been on a short voyage during the school holidays and would soon be leaving school.

The *Thomas Charles*

Lewis decided that he would sell some houses and buy a ship — the whole thing 64/64ths — the *Thomas Charles*, a schooner of 82-tons, built in Porthmadog in 1868 and, as he was the sole owner, he made his son, Robert, the master, under a sailing master, Robert Lewis of Aberdyfi. This was general practice at sea. Robert Lewis was an experienced sailing master. Bob, although called captain, was simply a pupil afloat, learning the 1,001 things about sailing, loading, navigating, even how to handle the crew. At the right time he would attend a marine school or college and try for his second mate's ticket, then progress to first mate and, eventually, become a fully qualified captain. At this stage, Robert Lewis would revert to first mate, but keep and eagle eye on his ex-pupil.

All three of Lewis Hughes's sons began their careers at sea on the *Thomas Charles* under Robert Lewis's tutorship. There was an understanding, however, that no more than two members of the family could be in the crew at the same time. This, no doubt, was to avoid the tragedy of a whole family of men being lost, as had happened too often in the past. When a third member of the family joined the crew, the second left for another ship.

Porthmadog was unique as a small port in having its own insurance company. Well set up and, because it had experienced ex-captains on its board, it had laid down sensible safety rules, which were strictly adhered to. Their inspector/surveyor was a retired captain who regularly visited the ships when they were in port. He also checked their 'insured' ships before they sailed, to ensure that the loading had been properly carried out, that sails and ropes were A1 (first class) and that food was adequate and plentiful. Should there be a wreck on shore, the inspector would visit to see whether salvage of any part was possible, or whether it was a total loss.

Another feature in Porthmadog was the bank, local yet international. Any captain who had a guarantee from the bank in his pocket, had no difficulty in getting cargo, food or repairs completed in any part of the world.

So it was that the *Thomas Charles* was fitted out, and the crew list for the second half of 1870, records the crew as being:

Robert Hughes	Master
Robert Lewis	Sailing Master
Henry Hughes	Able Seaman (brother of the Master and youngest son of Lewis Hughes)
William Williams	Ordinary Seaman
Griffith Williams	Mate
Hugh Hughes	Cook

Every six months, the master (or owner) had to outline the ship's plans for the coming half year in a log and, at the end of that period, give accurate details of where they had actually been; dates, details of cargo, etc. For some reason the *Thomas Charles* seems to report to the shipping master at Pwllheli. The voyage commencing 16 August 1871 shows the plan as being — 'By the month from Workington to Rotterdam and thence to any other Port wherever 'freight' may offer a voyage not to exceed six months'. This particular voyage proved to be a tragic one, as will be disclosed later.

Let me first give a few details about their ship — the *Thomas Charles*. This is how Aled Eames has it listed in his wonderful book *Porthmadog Ships*.

> *Thomas Charles*, schooner. Master; Robert Hughes son of Lewis Hughes the tailor at Porthmadog. 82 tons 69.5/20.0/10.7 [69.5 feet long, 20 feet wide and 10.7 feet deep]. Built 1868 by Griffiths, owned by Hughes & Co.

This little ship sailed to the Baltic ports, Labrador, Newfoundland, into the Mediterranean, to Italy, Greece and the ports of north Africa. No radar, no radio, no engine, simply accurate navigation using the sun and the stars. The ship was a well-built vessel, named after a famous preacher of the period, Thomas Charles from Bala, founder of the British & Foreign Bible Society. Mary, Lewis Hughes' wife, was a deeply religious woman but I don't think she had any influence in naming the ship. It had a figurehead of a preacher wearing a white 'dog-collar' with one arm raised, stressing a point — or in condemnation!

I have enquired widely, and searched shipping lists, but have not been able to find another ship named after a minister of religion. His peers constantly teased Robert, the young master, about the figurehead. He asked his parents if he could replace, it but his mother refused. Robert decided to do something about it and whenever he had a chance, gradually loosened the bolts and pins holding the figurehead to such an extent that, during a storm in the Bay of Biscay, it worked loose and Robert Lewis ordered it to be tied up. Later it was removed to the lazereet — a small hold in the bow for storing ropes and sundries. The figurehead was difficult to store so they hung it from the ceiling (which was the deck in this case).

When the ship arrived in Porthmadog, Robert's mother was upset to hear about the figurehead and blamed Robert but, when reassured by Robert Lewis that he had been obliged to remove it on safety grounds, she was pacified. However, that was not the end of the story, as you will hear later. For the time being the figurehead was replaced with a scroll and the *Thomas Charles* continued its busy schedule.

The 1871 voyage mentioned above, which began on 16 August 1871 from Workington, saw the ship destined for Rotterdam. During the unloading at the docks there, on 18 September, Robert Hughes, aged only 24, fell off the gangplank between the ship and quayside and was drowned. A few days later his body was recovered and was buried in Rotterdam. When Robert's body had surfaced, it was discovered by his youngest brother, Henry, who was emptying water from a boat that was tied to the stern of the *Thomas Charles*. It is difficult to imagine the trauma he must have suffered as he hung on to the bloated, possibly mutilated, body of his brother before help arrived. Detailed in the log of the *Thomas Charles* is the following statement:

On the 18th day of September 1871, Mr T. Spencer Reid, Pro Consul for the British Government in Rotterdam signed the Log Book of the *Thomas Charles* certifying that Robert Hughes, Master of the *Thomas Charles* had died by drowning in Rotterdam Harbour.

He also sanctioned the engagement of John Thomas, a qualified master (who happened to be at Rotterdam at the time), as temporary captain of the *Thomas Charles* for the return voyage. Eventually, the ship returned to Porthmadog with the temporary captain, John Thomas, in charge.

Lewis and Mary Hughes were deeply shocked by the death of their son and Mary felt particularly grieved that he was buried in a foreign land. She made arrangements for the *Thomas Charles* to take a cargo of slates to Genoa in Italy and from there to sail to Rotterdam, where they were to exhume Robert's body and bring him home for burial. Whilst in Genoa, they were to purchase a piece of Carrera marble suitable for Bob's gravestone. With the youngest son Harry Hughes as master, under the guidance of Robert Lewis, the *Thomas Charles* set sail for Genoa and, whilst there, obtained a gravestone before setting sail for Rotterdam where they got the necessary authority to exhume Bob's body and take it out of the country for re-burial. The coffin was placed in the lazareet of the *Thomas Charles*.

As they approached the English Channel, Robert Lewis, saw that the wind was rising and feared that it would get worse. He sent a sailor to the lazareet to get the 'double reef fairing', a long thin rope that was used to tie the sails tightly so that no wind could get into pockets and tear the sails. The sailor was a long time returning and someone was sent to look for him. The sailor was found lying on the deck with his candle lantern overturned and a small fire starting. When the man came-to he admitted that he was superstitious and was carefully skirting the coffin containing his former captain's body when he glanced upwards and there, staring down at him was Thomas Charles (the figurehead). Little wonder he fainted!

The rest of the journey home was uneventful. There was a crowd waiting at the dockside in Porthmadog when the ship docked and the cortége walked from the ship to the cemetery where his gravestone of Carrera marble is the only one in a 'forest' of slate.

Lewis and Mary Hughes were to suffer another tragedy when their second son, Hugh, was drowned in the *Catherine Richards* (a Porthmadog ship) when she sank with all hands in Brandon Bay, western Ireland, on 30 December 1891.

The youngest son Harry soon qualified and became one of the most famous captains of his period and is often mentioned in Aled Eames' books *Porthmadog Ships* and *Ships and Seamen of Anglesey* and also in *Immortal Sails* by Henry Hughes.

It is the story of Harry Hughes and his sons, in particular his eldest son, William Henry Hughes, that I will concentrate upon, for the simple reason that I married Elinor, Captain William Henry Hughes' eldest daughter, and spent many pleasant hours listening to his wonderful tales of the sea during his frequent visits to our home. His memory was fabulous up to the day of his death. I recorded many of his tales without his knowledge — but in time decided to record openly in order to be able to ask questions. He answered without any inhibitions at all. Unfortunately, recording conditions were not ideal, nor were the recording instrument or the operator of the highest standard.

Captain Harry Hughes

Captain Harry Hughes, the youngest son of Lewis and Mary Hughes married Jane Hope of 2 Harbour View, Caernarfon, and they had eight children: Mary (1884), William Henry (1886), Jesse (1889), Oswald (1891), Hubert (1893), Edith (1894), Arthur (1896) and Jennie (1900) — three girls and five boys. Four of the five boys followed in their father's footsteps and became sailors. Three of them captains, namely: William Henry, Jesse and Arthur. The eldest, William Henry, had the most dramatic and exciting career (although Jesse and Arthur also had great tales to tell of their dramatic lives at sea) and his story deserves to be re-told, if only to show the people of the twenty-first century how luxurious and easy their lives are compared to those of their predecessors of 100 years ago. Someone once coined the phrase 'men of steel and ships of wood'. This was that period and these men that they were referring to. They were often modest men who regarded a brave act as just another job which they were expected to do. Their pay was around £2 to £2 10s. (£2.50) per month. Some of the memorable events of Captain William Henry Hughes' career were:

Sailing around Britain with his father on the *Arvon* at only 12-years of age.

Being shipwrecked three times before reaching his eighteenth birthday.

Sailing around Cape Horn ten times, including the winter of 1905 when over 50 ships turned back.

Harry and Jenny Hughes, the parents of William Hughes.

Serving on the Irish Sea cross-channel boats during both the First and Second World Wars, when U-boats were a regular menace and many ships and lives were lost.

Being under fire during the Irish troubles in the 1920s.

Leading a party of sailors who successfully prevented the Irish Light Ship *Alexandra* being scuttled.

Receiving two Royal Humane Society Certificates on Vellum for bravery in rescuing people from the Irish Sea.

Being awarded the Distinguished Service Cross for bravery at Dunkirk in June, 1940.

The story itself is told mostly in his own words, from the tapes he had recorded over a period of years up to the mid 1980s.

Captain William Henry Hughes, DSC

I am Captain William Henry Hughes, a retired, square-rigged, master mariner, and at the request of my family and friends, I am going to relate some of my seafaring and other experiences.

I was born on the 24 August 1886 in Borth-y-gest. My father, Captain Henry Hughes, was a master mariner, born at Porthmadog, and my mother, Jane (Hope), was born at 2 Harbour View, Caernarfon, but lived with her grandmother at Morfa Bychan near Borth-y-gest. There were eight children in our family — five boys and three girls. Four of the brothers went to sea, and three of us became master mariners.

I went to Borth-y-gest Board School where the headmaster was Mr David Thomas, a noted historian and writer, a very gentle man who lacked discipline. As the school was crowded and took in boys and girls up to the age of 15, there was a great deal of quarrelling and fighting. It was not unusual to see a fight on the classroom floor. However, Mr Thomas was promoted to school inspector and was replaced as headmaster by Mr Hughes, a local man who had played football for Everton. We also had Mr Lynden Fielding as an extra teacher. Discipline was restored immediately. The new head also brought an Everton football for the boys to play with and thus expend their surplus energy.

I cannot remember much of my early school days beyond the fact that I learned to fight and it was the done thing to challenge and be challenged. I became quite a good boxer. I recall once fighting my best friend Bob Roberts simply because he had challenged me. My mother was unaware of my boxing until she asked my brother Jesse why I was late from school only to be told. 'Oh he is in the field by school accepting challenges to fight. He'll beat them all.'

We were given a day off when a ship was launched in either Porthmadog or Borth-y-gest. These launchings usually took place in spring, during the high tides. I recall two ships being launched on the same day. The one from David Williams' yard was launched sideways like the Liberty ships in America fifty years later; the other was launched stern first as usual. Two paddle tugs, the *Snowdon* and the *Wave of Life*, were ready to take them in tow to the dockside for final fitting of sails, ropes, furniture and hundreds of other things before the ships were ready to be checked by the insurance assessors.

There was plenty of wood and soft soap lying around after the launch and the children and parents carried most of it away no doubt to save the best pieces of wood and burn the rest. No doubt the soap was also put to good use. I can also remember the *Consul Kaestner* being launched from the little station. There was always a platform for the important guest and owners and often a brass band or a choir to entertain the hundreds gathered around. As soon as the ship had been launched they prepared the site for the keel of another.

As my father was captain of a ship using the harbour, I was allowed on the docks and I used to enjoy watching the blacksmiths, carpenters and other tradesmen at work. One such tradesman was Evan Morgan who made fine furniture for the new ships. He was also a fine musician and singer, well known as 'Llew Madog'. He composed several hymn tunes, including my favourite 'Tyddyn Llwyn'. One day, I called to see him but he was having lunch and I passed the time testing his chisels. Later that afternoon, a friend told me to hide as Llew Madog was after my blood. When I asked why, he replied, 'Not only did you play with his tools, but you cut your initials 'W.H.H.' on a lovely piece of mahogany destined for the captain's desk on that ship.' I did not see Llew Madog for some time.

Another memory I have, is of trays of food and buckets of soup and tea, being carried into the Town Hall to feed many soldiers in uniform, who were the Volunteer Fusiliers who were called in for any special event. Later many of them went off to fight in the Boer War. Years later I was sailing home through the Bay of Biscay, when the 'lookout' reported that there were hundreds of strange objects in the water ahead. From a distance we assumed they were a jellyfish, called the 'Portuguese Man-of-War', but when we came up to them they turned out to be hundreds of 'pith' helmets, thrown overboard by soldiers returning from the Boer War when they were told to change back into their cold weather uniforms.

My father was the son of a master tailor named Lewis Hughes. I recall him as a tall, well-dressed man with a rather thin, piping voice, who was also very interested in shipping. He had bought a ship called the *Thomas Charles*, as an investment, and his three sons; Robert, Hugh and Henry all sailed on her. Robert, the eldest, was the master on the *Thomas Charles* under Robert Lewis, a sailing master from Aberdyfi. Robert sailed widely, often with one of his two brothers as a crew member. Unfortunately Captain Robert was drowned in Rotterdam in September 1871. My father, Henry (or Harry as he was called) was only a young man, but took over the ship under the same sailing master, Mr Robert Lewis of Aberdyfi, until he qualified himself as a master mariner.

After a while, Lewis Hughes decided to invest more in shipping and had built for himself a 3-masted schooner called the *Hilda*, a Newfoundland trader, and my father took command of her and sailed her for 18 months to two years before they built another ship called the *Edward Seymour* (with my father and grandfather holding all the shares).

The *Edward Seymour*

The *Edward Seymour* was a barquentine and my father again took command of her and sailed her all over the Baltic, to North and South America, India, South Africa, Argentina, Canada and the Mediterranean. He sailed into the north African ports long before the Elder Dempster Shipping Company started going there.

The Edward Seymour. *[GAS XS/690/3/10]*

My father also managed to get government contracts taking cargo to various islands and dependencies. He traded to St Helena and Ascension Island, then to Cape Town and on to the West Indies carrying vital supplies and bringing sugar, or whatever product they had, back to Dublin or Liverpool, or wherever it was needed. He had sailed to the South African ports of Cape Town, Durban and on to Calcutta. In fact, they were just building Durban when he first went there and he was offered a post as the first harbourmaster.

In a two year period with the *Edward Seymour* he sailed: Dublin to Malaga, Portugal, Madeira, Antwerp, Köningsberg, the Black Sea, Corunna, Cardiff, Tunis, West Indies, France, Sicily, Baltic, Azoff Sea, Holland, Azores, Canary Islands, U.S.A. (between Eastport and Galveston), the West Indies, Brazil, the River Plate, Uruguay, Glasgow, Berbice, North America, Tobago, eastern coast of North, Central and South America, the St Lawrence, the River Plate, back to Cardiff and then to Tenerife, St Thomas (Dutch West

Facing: The Agreement and Account of Crew for the Edward Seymour, *showing the owner's name as Lewis Hughes.*

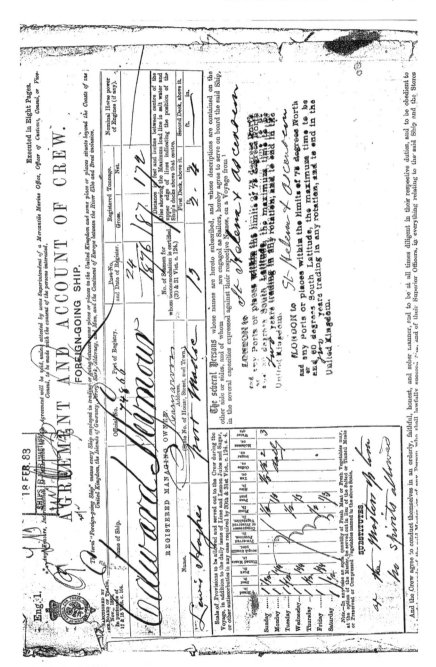

Indies), Puerto Rico, Troon to Demerara, Curaçoa, Caernarfon to Hamburg, Helsingborg, Dunkirk, St Helena, Ascension Islands, Trinidad, Barbados, Cape of Good Hope, Natal, Calcutta, Pernambuco, Buenos Aires, Halifax (Nova Scotia), Stettin, Natal, Rio Grande, Rosario, Rouen, St Nicholas, the River Plate, Nijkerk and back to Porthmadog. All these places, in all kinds of weather, in a barquentine of 187 tons with sails only, no engine, no radio, no satellite navigation and a crew of five or six.

Small wonder that after many years of long trips, some lasting well over two years, he decided he wanted shorter voyages so he could spend more time with his growing family. He sold his shares in the *Edward Seymour* and, as his father had another ship called the *Geraldine*, took command of her. That ship only traded to the Baltic and round the coast of northern Europe on fairly short voyages. He was on the *Geraldine* for some time, until she foundered off the Pembrokeshire coast. After that, he bought shares in another ship called the *Edwin*, and traded to Newfoundland and the Mediterranean. This was a regular run for Porthmadog ships, which I shall tell you about later. He was on the *Edwin* for a few years before he bought another schooner called the *Arvon*, and that brings it to my time.

The *Arvon*

In July 1898, I first went to sea on the *Arvon*. I was almost 12-years old. The ship had been bought in Caernarfon and I happened to be starting on my school holidays. My father asked me if I would like to make a pleasure voyage with him. I was delighted, as it was the only life that I, and the boys of Borth-y-Gest School, ever considered.

Now that I think about it, it was not my first voyage. When my father first bought the *Edward Seymour*, my mother had gone on a short voyage and taken me with her as a baby in her arms. But I cannot remember any of that trip.

Facing: The Edwin. *[GAS XS/1279/7/207e]*

I went by train from Porthmadog to Caernarfon and was seen off by my mother and my brothers and sisters. All were ready with advice and good wishes, especially my mother, who warned me more than anything to keep out of the way of the men at work, and to keep away from danger, not to climb the masts, and so on. After what seemed ages, the train drew into Caernarfon Station, but I'd already had a glimpse of the ships loading slate at the quayside just before the train entered the tunnel under the town square.

It did not take me long to get from the station to my grandmother's house, which was almost on the seafront, opposite the Anglesey Arms. The houses were near the castle, and in fact, I thought that the castle was in my grandmother's back garden. Sadly the little group of houses were all pulled down in the late 1960s.

Grandmother Hope had a meal ready for me, but I was more anxious to see the new ship. However she insisted that I ate something, knowing that I would not come off the ship to eat, nor would they have time to feed me on board. She also insisted that I changed into my old clothes, knowing full well that they would be dirty and torn before the voyage had even begun. At last I was allowed to run up the quayside to look for the *Arvon*.

The quayside was a hive of activity. Not only were there wagons of slates from different quarries in the Nantlle Valley, but also horses and carts carrying goods from local shops, farms and factories, delivering food and various items for the journeys, and also for shops in Liverpool and elsewhere. There seemed to be hundreds of people around, just like the docks at Porthmadog, everyone seemed to know what to do. I soon found the *Arvon* loading slates for South Shields.

My father took a moment or two off to welcome me, and then warned me to stand clear, but to watch and learn how all the loaders and others did their job. Loading slates is a skilled and painstaking job; it can also be dangerous as the edges can be as sharp as a knife. Nobody will accept broken slates and so it was very important that they all reached their destination in one piece.

After completing the loading, each ship was moved further down the river in order to allow another ship to come against the quayside to load. This was in July of 1898, two years before the Aber Bridge was built in 1900/1. The only way across was by ferry using one of Dafydd yr Aber's boats. Any movement of ships to or from the quayside had to be by manpower. Ships sailed in on the tide as near as possible to their loading point, and that depended on which quarry was involved.

At that time, there was no tugboat in Caernarfon, so to move a ship up or down river meant manhandling, because there were other ships, masts and spars in the way. There were men in boats pulling or pushing. Others ashore were releasing or tying ropes on to bollards because the river and the tide made unusual currents. It would be dreadful to damage the ship or the cargo before starting from Caernarfon.

After loading, they tied up the ship a little further down river to wait for the right tide. When this happened they called on the 'Hobblers'. These were a group of 8 or 10 men who picked up this long strong rope, tied to the ship, and they pulled her alongside the Town Wall (known locally as 'The South of France'). When they got 'near the 'Battery' they had to put extra effort and run so that the ship could then get enough speed, drop the rope and veer out towards the deep water of the Menai Straits. There, they would anchor until the weather and tide were right for them to cross the bar between Anglesey and Caernarfon by Belan Fort.

For their efforts each 'hobbler' would get a card and on it was written *Cortyn Peint* (Pint Cord) with the name of the ship. This entitled the bearer to a pint of beer in the 'Vaynol Arms'. Soon afterwards a tugboat came to Caernarfon and the 'Hobblers' and the *Cortyn Peint* were no longer needed.

After a few days wind bound, we eventually sailed over Caernarfon bar. The wind being southerly we went 'northabout' for Scotland and South Shields. After sailing into the Irish Sea I cannot remember much, nor did I see very much, because I was terribly seasick, but I do remember my father calling me on deck in the middle of the night to see Rathlin Islands off Northern Ireland because a Porthmadog ship had been wrecked there. We proceeded north and had a lot of bad weather. We had to put in to Stornway for repairs because the lower topsail yard had been carried away.

We were there a few days and then proceeded north through the Pentland Firth and that was quite an experience. My father held the boat back until the tide was just right then shouted, 'Now!' and, as the crew followed his orders, the *Arvon* went through the Pentland Firth at speed, and came out the other side like a cork from a bottle. We eventually reached South Shields, where we discharged our cargo of slate Then my father was offered a cargo of coal, so we proceeded to Hepburn on Tyne to load gas coal for Skibereen in southern Ireland.

Skibereen is on the south-west corner of Ireland, and at the entrance is a little port called Baltimore, a very nice little place. Skibereen itself is well up the river and had no dock, so we anchored in the river and lighters (barges) unloaded the coal. I went with my father to see the merchant and the gas works. What surprised me then as a boy of twelve was that the gasworks manager was a Mr Owen, a Welsh-speaking Welshman.

After discharging the coal we loaded ballast and sailed back to Porthmadog. The voyage being over, I went back to school the very next day. Although the term had started over a month previously, no one told me off and I stayed on in school for the winter but was determined to become a sailor and see more of the world, in spite of the sea-sickness.

In the summer of 1899, I started properly at sea having signed on as an ordinary seaman with my father on the *Arvon*. We sailed one coasting voyage to Portsmouth and back to Porthmadog and, although I suffered seasickness, I enjoyed myself. The next voyage was to Bremen then on to a port on the south coast before returning to Porthmadog. Our final voyage on the *Arvon* was to Perth in

Scotland. We came to a little place called Dyshart, a few miles from Dundee, where we loaded coal for a place in Norway called Tonsburg.

We had a variety of weather — good and bad — and arrived in Tonsburg where we discharged our coal then sailed to Frederickstaad in Norway to load timber for Porthmadog. After loading the timber we set off but had very bad weather again and had to put into a little place called Gamble Helleston, a creek where we sheltered for a few days. The bad weather continued in the North Sea, it was rough there for days on end, but as it was December it was to be expected. Eventually, we reached Yarmouth Roads and Gorleston Roads.

After a day or so of heavy south-east gales, we were driven ashore onto the beach and the *Arvon* became a total wreck. The ship listed inwards and the sea was coming over but with the big deck cargo of timber we were sheltered. This later altered and the cargo was scattered all over the place. The two masts went over the side with the ship listing out. We sent off rocket signals of distress and we could soon see the coastguards signalling that they had seen us. It was between three and four in the morning but we could see lights on the shore and the coastguards began to fire rockets (for the breeches buoy). We managed to get hold of the rope on the second or third attempt and heaved in the hawser (rope). As we had no mast, we tied it to the highest place we could. The lack of height caused us to be in water from the time we left the ship until we reached the shore.

I, being the youngest, was first into the bosun's chair. I accidentally put both legs down one hole without realising! It was wet and dark and I was constantly under water. I remember eventually getting ashore almost drowned and there were hundreds of people around. I remember looking at a bucket with steam rising from it; and later was told that it was hot wine that had been sent from the large house at the top of the cliff belonging to Mr Colman, the mustard manufacturer. He also sent horses and carts to take us to the sailors' home in Lowestoft. There were no cars available in those days.

After getting dry clothes and food, we stayed a day and were then sent home to Porthmadog. That was December 1899 — about a fortnight before Christmas — and was my first shipwreck.

My father then went for a voyage on a schooner called the *Frau Mina Peterson*, sailing for Stettin in the Baltic. There was a great deal of ice and they had to put into a harbour in Norway to wait for the ice to clear. It was very cold weather. I would have liked to have gone with him, but I had to go back to school for that winter.

Before he came back, I had left school and had shipped in a little schooner called *Faith* as cook and ordinary seaman and we sailed for St Helen's, in the Isle of Wight and from there to Fareham and then up with a cargo of china clay for Lancaster. I should tell you here that very few ports had 'dockers' in those days, Almost all the loading and unloading was done by the crew. Some cargo was easy, but clay was heavy and dirty, but the worst cargo we had to deal with was guano, but more of that later.

The *Miss Pritchard*

My father had bought another schooner called the *Miss Pritchard* so I left the *Faith* at Lancaster and came home to go with him on the *Miss Pritchard*. I sailed a number of voyages with him around the coast and some to the Baltic, Bremen, Copenhagen, Hamburg and up to Norway. The last voyage I made with the *Miss Pritchard* was as an ordinary seaman. We had come from Norway to Pwllheli with a cargo of timber, discharged the timber there and took in ballast then sailed to Cadiz in Spain, where we loaded salt for Newfoundland.

We set sail for a place called Bay Roberts on the coast of St John's, Newfoundland. After discharging salt for the fishermen, we were sent up the coast of Labrador to discharge more salt at different ports. In going up we had experienced fog and there were a lot of icebergs around, small, but very dangerous. I remember one day in

The Frau Mina Peterson. *[GAS XS/1279/7/132e]*

The Miss Pritchard. *[GAS XS/195/14]*

particular. There was no wind but thick fog. All of a sudden there was a huge iceberg upon us. We had heard the noise of ice breaking off and falling into the sea, so we knew it was fairly near, and then we saw it only a few feet from us. We thought once that we would run into it but the current took us slowly past. By evening, the icebergs had cleared and we got to a little harbour called Pinsondarms — by Cape Charles. There is a little creek there where we discharged 50 tons of salt for the fishermen and sailed on to another place called Bateaux, where there were a few Porthmadog ships tied up.

After a few days we had to go to a place called Domino Run, where we discharged the rest of our salt. The fishermen were out all night catching our cargo of fish. As soon as they landed, everybody set-to gutting the fish, and then they laid them out on the rocks, salted them and left them to dry. The fish were then packed into barrels, and loaded on our ship. We were in Newfoundland for over three weeks.

Whilst we were there, I heard of another ship called the *Dorothy* lying about two-and-a-half miles from us so I decided to walk over to this creek to see them as I knew some of the crew. I went on my own and had tea with them. It gets dark very early there and before I realised, it was quite dark, although only around 5 o'clock. As there was no proper road, just paths over the rocks, I was a bit concerned that I would get back safely. By the time I started back it was really dark. The fishermen used to employ Eskimos to work during the fishing season and they then went back up north to their igloo villages. All of them had dogs called huskies, and I shall never forget that night, as I was never more scared than when going back in the dark over those dangerous rocky paths, without any light, and hearing these dogs howling and barking nearby. I was really glad to see the lights of my ship at Domino Run.

The ship was almost completely loaded but an iceberg had been reported nearby for two weeks or more and it was feared that it might block the harbour we were in and then we'd be there for the winter. The fishermen were loading as fast as they could, but one Sunday, they reckoned that there was grave danger of the blockage happening. All were rather distressed about it, so we decided to sail with what we had already loaded.

On that Sunday morning it was blowing a whole gale, fair wind for us, so we reefed the mainsail, foresail and topsail and sailed before the gale. There were several icebergs around that night and it was still blowing hard. The captain (my father) decided that he would not run before the wind any more and hove the ship to.

There was an iceberg about half-a-mile from us, which, more or less, sheltered us although it drifted near and a few lumps of ice fell on the deck, but did no harm. The morning was fine so we set full sail for Gibraltar for orders, and got there in 16 days — a very good passage. After being there two to three days, we were ordered to Malaga to discharge the fish. Then we sailed in ballast to Larache in Morocco — rather an awkward place to enter but very snug after getting in.

We anchored outside the port and a big tug came out to tow us. All the hatches and skylights had to be closed — the living quarters sealed and everything to be as watertight as possible as we had to enter through huge Atlantic rollers on the bar. The crew had to climb up the rigging and the helmsman (father) was lashed to the wheel. As we went through, everything was covered with water. Even we, up the rigging were soaked and had to hang on for grim death, but once through we were in calm waters and, as I said, in a very snug port. I recall looking down at my father, but there was nothing to be seen but water then, suddenly, he emerged, with water still flowing from his bushy red beard.

We loaded beans there for Falmouth and whilst we were there, orders came for us to go to Irvine in Scotland to discharge and pick up a load of coal. We had a very rough passage from Morocco, with particularly heavy gales in the Bay of Biscay. Many days were spent hove-to, but the ship was a good sea boat so it did not disturb us very much. Eventually, we got to Falmouth on Christmas Eve

1900. After sailing to Irvine we returned to Porthmadog and unloaded the cargo of coal. My brother Jesse was now ready to go to sea, so I had to leave the *Miss Pritchard* and I joined another fine schooner called the *Nesta* and sailed with that ship to Bremen, then Dublin, and after a couple of voyages we returned to Porthmadog.

The *Cambria*

Whilst in Porthmadog waiting for a cargo, I decided to go on another ship and so joined a little schooner called the *Cambria* which carried a cargo of around 150-tons and had a crew of three, plus the captain. The ship was loading slate for Kilrush — not far from Limerick on the Shannon. We sailed from Porthmadog and, after discharging the slate, we were there for about ten days loading kelp for Bowline, near Glasgow in Scotland. The mate, who was a Russian/Finn, and the captain, fell out, so Captain Roberts paid him off. Now there were only two of us left, the captain and myself, when there should be a crew of three and the captain. He, Captain Roberts, was a big, tall fellow, but rather fond of the drink! I did not see him for days on end, so I used to go to look for him. Eventually, he came back on the Saturday afternoon with two or three boatmen and said he'd decided to sail.

We sailed out of Kilrush and anchored outside the harbour — about a quarter-of-a-mile from the pier (there was nothing to pay out there). Then he went off again with these boatmen and told me to bring the boat ashore to fetch him about nine o'clock. I was alone then until nine when I went ashore, but there was no sign of him. I waited until eleven o'clock, but still there was no sign of him. The tide was getting strong and there were no lights on the ship, so I had to go back to her and set the anchor lights. As there was no sign of Captain Roberts I decided to go to bed, after giving the ship more chain.

The next morning, Sunday, he came aboard with plenty of food (he was a kind old fellow, no shortage of anything). He slept all day that Sunday and at six o'clock on the Monday morning he was up shouting that we were going to sail — just the two of us! We hoisted all the sail and set off down the Shannon and round the south coast and did very well. Only two of us taking 'spell about'. One of us would steer whilst the other cooked or rested, but I think he must have done most of the steering because it was hard work with a tiller, and I used to get very tired. The old man used to enjoy being at the tiller because he used to sing, he was always singing, and singing hymns at that. I believe he was a good singer.

We had mixed weather during the crossing, and then by Bardsey Island we had very bad weather — westerly and south-westerly. We were tacking by the lightship in Cardigan Bay and the captain had been a long time on the tiller, so he called me to give him a spell and put her head out to sea and told me to take over, as he was going for a rest. It was quite easy to hold her in the one direction, towards Ireland, and as I was almost above his cabin skylight I could easily call him if required. He hadn't been down long before the topsail halyards were carried away and I shouted to him. He asked, 'Is it drawing?' in Welsh, but, before I could answer, the staysail halyard was also carried away. He came up and told me to haul it down, so I pulled the mainsail down.

The next afternoon we got to Holyhead wind-bound and anchored there. There were a number of ships moored there and it was a Saturday, so off he went ashore to get more stores. He came back very late that night, singing as ever. On Sunday morning I was fast asleep when he called me for breakfast at 8 a.m. He was dressed in his very creased frock coat and a hat, and said that he was going to chapel. I asked if I could go with him but he refused because he had some tasks for me to do and off he went with some men from one of the other ships. I spent my Sunday rowing backwards and forwards to the *Corby Castle*, one of the other ships, to bring five bags of coal that he had bought off the captain. Following that, I had to fill our tank with fresh water from the huge tank of water that used to be on the front by the old lifeboat hut on Newry Beach. We had no coal from Kilrush, only peat, which wasn't very good, as it burned too quickly.

After anchoring for a few days in Holyhead, the wind turned favourable and Captain Roberts decided to sail for Bowline with just the two of us. We fell out over heaving the anchor because he was so much stronger than me. He had rigged up a windlass to help raise the anchor and other heavy things. Unfortunately, because of his strength, the handle caught me under the chin and knocked me out. He complained that I wasn't pulling my weight, so I refused duty and sat down on my bed. He tried coaxing and threatening alternately and, eventually, we became friends.

We hauled the anchor and sailed, taking turnabout on the tiller. Eventually, we arrived on the Clyde, but there were strong headwinds, and while I was holding the topsail yards up, the 'chain swing' from the boat broke and fell on my shoulder. It hurt me so badly that I could not help with the tacking of the ship. I took the tiller and he tacked the ship himself all the way up to Greenock. He pulled the yards round and did the work of three men all by himself. All I had to do was steer. We eventually got a tug to take us to Bowline where we discharged our cargo. After a day or two he went off again and I didn't see him for days.

I decided I wasn't going any further on this ship and I wanted to be paid off, but there was nobody to pay me off. I had made friends with the mate on a ship from the Isle of Man who wished to give me a job on his ship and so I was expecting Captain Roberts back. But he didn't come for days. When he did come back, I waited until we were having tea, but I could tell that he'd been around Glasgow, and had spent most of the freight money.

It was an oval table, I was at one end and he the other, and I was going to tell him that I'd made up my mind to leave. Eventually I told him that I wanted to be paid off. I must have sounded timid, because he didn't say anything so I repeated it, louder (and in Welsh of course). He looked up at me and said, 'No I won't pay you off, what would your father say if I did pay you off here?' So that was it. Someone told me 'If you see a customs officer, repeat the request before him, and he can compel him to pay you off.' I saw the customs officer and told him. He said, 'Well, the ship is under 70 tons and is not on the register, nor have you signed any agreement so I have no authority to force him but I will speak to him.' He evidently had a word with him because I was paid off with 38s. My pay was 30s. per month. Old Captain Roberts did not like it at all; in fact, there were tears in his eyes when I left him.

I went down to Greenock to join a steamer going to Liverpool, a passenger boat. We should have left at midnight and arrive at Liverpool at 8 a.m. but there was fog and we didn't get in until noon. I was going towards Lime Street to catch a train home when I saw the white masts of a huge ship in Salthouse Dock. I entered the dock for a closer look and discovered it was the *Pengwern* (William Thomas), a full-rigged ship.

The ship was light and high so I put my bag down and climbed aboard. I had remembered that the chief officer was Mr Jones from Borth-y-Gest, (my home). I went towards the galley where the cook, in white clothes, asked what I wanted. I told him I wished to see Mr Jones. He said he was in bed (Sunday afternoon) and could not be disturbed.

I talked with this man for about an hour or so, then I saw Mr Jones walking on the poop deck. He saw me and beckoned me up. He asked where I'd come from and so on and then said, 'You won't get a train until 11 p.m. so come and have tea with me,' which I did. He was going to Princes Road Chapel so he offered to take me to Lime Street, but it was too early so I went to look around Liverpool after leaving my bag in the Left Luggage. Before leaving he asked if I would like to join the *Pengwern* as ordinary seaman as there was a vacancy for the trip to Melbourne Australia, I said I would be delighted. 'Well we won't be sailing for three weeks or more so enjoy your holiday'.

I got the 11 p.m. train from Lime Street Liverpool and got home to Borth-y-gest in the early morning. My father was away, so after breakfast I told my mother about meeting Mr Jones and how I'd

The George Casson. *[GAS XS/690/4a/39]*

accepted his offer to sail on the *Pengwern* to Melbourne. She said she'd never heard of the *Pengwern* and when I praised the big lovely ship with a local man as chief officer, I thought she'd be happy. But, when she realised that Melbourne was in Australia, she said, 'No you cannot go all that way — Hamburg is far enough for anyone'. And that was that.

I then joined the brigantine *George Casson*; Captain Lewis of Bron Afon, Borth-y-gest was captain and I was very happy on her for a couple of voyages. Just before my third voyage I was taken ill with tonsillitis. This was towards the end of 1902.

The *Excelsior*

When I'd got over the illness, the ship had sailed. A pilot came with a message from Captain Evans of the *Excelsior* who was asking to see me. I went to Porthmadog to see him and was offered a berth as ordinary seaman on the very nice brig, the *Excelsior*, and I sailed in her with part cargo for Copenhagen and Kiel.

Headwinds held us up in St Tudwal's Roads then we continued to Falmouth to avoid strong winds and found a nice, sheltered anchorage but a big tug came to shift us to make room for some warships. When the weather was suitable, we sailed to Kiel on the Elbe. The ship was leaking badly and the eight hands had to do a lot of pumping. I was in the mate's watch — an old man called Mr Griffith from Caernarfon. Eventually we arrived in Kiel through the canal and discharged part cargo.

It was very cold as we sailed through the very narrow waters to Copenhagen and discharged the remainder of the cargo. The ship had been chartered to go on to Halmstaad in Sweden, to load paving stones for southern England, I don't remember exactly where. This meant going backwards and forwards in the Baltic in thick weather and eventually we got into the harbour in a fierce gale. During the night it developed into a hurricane. There was an anchor watch that the mate had put on. The first watch was from 10 till 12. I was to watch from 12 till 2. At midnight, the pilot was about and he told me in broken English, 'I vos in hurricanes and typhoons and all kinds of phoons, but never I see anything like this'. He had failed to get ashore because it was blowing so hard.

The Excelsior. *[GAS XS/690/4a/78]*

The mate had said, 'If you find the anchor dragging call 'All Hands' at once.' I had my foot on the cable and was watching some lights ashore. At about one o'clock I thought she was dragging so I called 'All Hands!' and ran aft for Captain Evans. We parted the chain and drifted ashore and sank on the shore. Christmas Eve 1902 was spent in the rigging of the *Excelsior* in a hurricane off Halmstad in Sweden.

Luckily, the tide was ebbing and we didn't have to leave the ship, but she was filled with water and was a total wreck. After a few days we were sent home on a passenger ship of the Wilson Line from Halmstaad to Hull. The chief steward was not too happy to have us on his ship and put us in the steerage, saying that we had to pay for our food. Our mate went to see the purser, saying that even pigs were entitled to food. The purser told the chief steward to find us cabins and ensure we had ample food.

Eventually we arrived in Hull and again there was trouble. At that time the owner was not supposed to pay shipwrecked sailors beyond the first port. This rule has since been changed to homeport or the port you signed on at. At Hull some were short of money, but as I had been shipwrecked before, and had joined the Fisherman's Society I was entitled to money for loss of clothes, passage, etc. Six of us got to the Board of Trade office and asked for our fare home. They asked us if any of us belonged to the Fishermen & Shipwrecked Sailors' Society — I was the only one, so they gave me my fare and food money. He then turned to the others and said, 'Seeing that you are destitute, we'll pay your fare on condition you drink one pint of beer a month less, to pay for joining the Society (beer was 3*d*. a pint and the Fishermen's Society was 3*s*. a year).

I must say we enjoyed our Christmas Day in Halmstaad. They looked after us very well. That was my second shipwreck.

The *David Morris*
On arrival in Porthmadog I was fitted out with new clothes, etc. and I joined the three-masted schooner called the *David Morris* — a

fine ship, and sailed in her to Copenhagen direct and we went round the Skaw this time, not through the canal. We were supposed to go on to Newfoundland but eventually went to Frederickstaad and loaded timber for Aberdyfi. Then we were to be towed to Porthmadog for reclassification before going to Newfoundland. All hands were paid off, but, as I was living in Borth-y-gest, I was kept on. After breakfast at home, I had dinner with Captain Morris in his house.

One day, the captain's wife showed me a huge silk scarf or handkerchief and said her father was Captain Lewis of the *Confidence* and he had been given the scarf by General Garibaldi, the Italian leader, when he had saved Garibaldi from his enemies. He had come aboard when trying to escape from Italy, and pleaded with Captain Lewis to hide him. Although he was putting his own life, and maybe the lives of his crew and his ship at risk, Captain Lewis decided to help him. The mainsail was furled so Garibaldi was put to lie on the boom and the mainsail was rolled tightly about him. No sooner had they hidden him, than the troops from

The schooner David Morris. *[GAS XS/2129.7e]*

the following warship searched the *Confidence* — but failed to find him. On arrival in Plymouth, Garibaldi gave him his silk scarf and a baton saying, 'You saved my life, I have only these to give you. I saw the ship's name, *Confidence*, and that inspired me to come aboard. Thank you'.

Many years later I was retired and travelling home from Liverpool by train. In the carriage were two other men. The *Liverpool Daily Post* had been running an article on Garibaldi a week or two previously. We got to Chester and a Captain Wright and another gentleman joined us. They were talking and one of them said he was an officer with the Cunard. Captain Wright turned to me and said — 'We have met before somewhere'. I told him I was Captain of the *Hibernia*, one of the Holyhead to Dublin ferries. That started a conversation about one of my officers, a Mr Phillips. Then he said he'd been to the outward bound school in Aberdyfi, run by Alfred Holt. The school's sailing ship was called the *Garibaldi* and I said I'd seen her coming into Holyhead in distress years ago, when Commander Villiers was in charge, and I had met him and chatted about his books and, as we had both sailed in square riggers, we had a great deal to talk about.

Captain Wright said, 'I was sent to Aberdyfi to entertain some lord who was a friend of Alfred Holt. He had instructed me to sit next to him and regale him with sea stories.'

I then told him my story about Captain Lewis of the *Confidence* rescuing Garibaldi and the story of the silk scarf. 'Well', he said, 'I wish I'd had that story to tell the lord. He would have been delighted.' At that stage another of the passengers in the carriage said, 'Do you know where that scarf is now?'

'No', I replied.

'Well, I have it in my home in Cemaes. My wife wanted me to write to the *Daily Post* at the time — but I didn't bother'.

I often wondered who that man was, as I did not get his name at the time.

To go back to my early days, after leaving the *David Morris*, I went on the *Sarah Evans* as an able seaman. My friend, Robert Roberts (later a captain in Q-ships), was also an able seaman on her. His father was the captain and we sailed for Esbjerg in Denmark, and from there to Gottenberg, where we loaded timber for Pwllheli.

Back to the *Miss Pritchard*

Following that voyage, I joined my father and brother Jesse again on the *Miss Pritchard* as an able seaman. Later, I was promoted mate. We sailed for Copenhagen from Porthmadog, going northabout, and had to put into Stornoway for repairs after bad weather. We stayed for a few days but, after leaving, we had more bad weather. The ship began to leak and eventually foundered ten miles north of Cape Wrath. We had to abandon ship and take to the boats, rowing towards the lighthouse in very heavy seas. When we got there, the keepers pointed us to a creek nearby where we could land. They gave us hot food and we had our clothes dried.

As the weather improved, we launched the boat and had to pull on our oars another 15 miles to Lochinver. After being there three to four days a coastal steamer picked us up and took us to Mallaig and Oban where we got a train to Glasgow and eventually on to Porthmadog. That was my last voyage in Porthmadog ships and it was August 1904. I was almost 18 years old, and had been shipwrecked three times!

It was time to travel further in bigger ships and visit new countries. There was a large Porthmadog ship, too large to enter the harbour, but owned and run by a local company, Pritchard Brothers. She was the *Beeswing*. Her details: steel barque, 1,462 tons 236.5/ 36/ 21.7. Built by Russell & Co Greenock, 1893. Owned by Beeswing Sailing Ship Company. (Pritchard Bros & Co) Captain R. Griffith, Master.

The *Beeswing*

I wanted to go into deep water to get my certificates, so I joined the barque *Beeswing*, a Porthmadog ship but it was too big to come into Porthmadog harbour. I joined it at Rotterdam with Captain Griffiths, Aberdaron, as master, and Mr Owen Owens of Borth-y-gest as first mate. We were sailing round the Horn to Newcastle, Australia, and then on to the Guano Islands off Chile. Every sailor had heard tales of the dreadful weather to be experienced around Cape Horn, and each one also hoped that it would be better weather for his journey.

This was my first trip over the Equator and we had the usual 'fun' ceremony of 'Crossing the Line.' Neptune came aboard, having been lowered over the side — dressed appropriately and carrying a trident. He asked if there were any sailors crossing for the first time and, as I was one of them, I was dragged forward for the ceremony. There was plenty of grease, soot, soap and water about, with everybody singing and shouting. I knew that it was best to keep my mouth tightly shut or it would be filled with soapy

The Porthmadog barque Beeswing. *[GAS XS1279/7/127e]*

BARQUE 'BEESWING'
'Full and Bye' Starboard Tack

1 Flying Jib

2 Outer Jib

3 Inner Jib

4 Foretopmast Staysail

5 Fore Royal Sail

6 Fore Top Gallant Sail

7 Fore Upper Top Sail
(Reef Points)

8 Fore Lower Top Sail

9 Fore Course (Reef Points)

10 Main Royal Sail

11 Main Top Gallant Sail

12 Main Upper Topsail
(Reef Points)

13 Main Lower Topsail

14 Main Course (Reef Points)

15 Mizzen Gaff Topsail

16 Spanker

17 Main Royal Staysail

18 Main Topmast Staysail

19 Main Staysail

20 Mizzen Topmast Staysail

21 Mizzen Top Gallant Staysail

22 Mizzen Staysail

water. Similarly, anyone who raised any objection got far worse treatment. I just accepted everything and enjoyed myself. The ship's carpenter and the sailmaker had certainly been busy preparing for this event.

We had very mixed weather all the way, from storms in the Bay of Biscay to total stillness in the Doldrums, and then constant westerly and south-westerly winds round the Horn. I had never seen such waves as we encountered below 50 degrees south and the wind was bitterly cold with sheets and sails frozen solid.

As we came to the 50 degree south line, all hands were busy changing into heavy weather sails, ropes, etc. Everything that could move was lashed or put safely away. Safety lines were fixed along the decks and all the crew who had not previously rounded the Horn were told how and 'how not' to use them. If we had been doubtful about the value of these precautions beforehand, we were certainly convinced a few days later after the crossing which took the *Beeswing* over six weeks to clear the Horn and turn northwards.

We had cargo for Newcastle, Australia and on arrival were given a great welcome. In his classic book *The War with Cape Horn*, Captain Alan Villiers describes 1905 as the worst ever period to sail around the Horn. This is based upon the logs and crew agreements of the sailing ships, which battled around the Horn in 1905. He describes it as 'particularly difficult for ships bound for the west coast of Chile or California. Many ships were lost — they simply disappeared. During that winter, 40–50 ships had to turn away and run in distress for the Falklands, Montevideo or Rio, to lick their wounds and return to fight again. Over a dozen ships gave up altogether, choosing to run right round and sail eastwards round the Cape of Good Hope with, they hoped, the gales behind them'. The *Beeswing* was one ship that made it round the Horn in 1905.

There were always strikes at Newcastle, which delayed us rather, but we were given a great welcome and were pleased to be lazing in warm weather after the rigours of Cape Horn. From Newcastle the *Beeswing* sailed to the Guano Islands to load guano. Filthy, evil-smelling stuff that burned your skin, particularly between your fingers and toes. There was no port or pier to moor, so we were anchored out to sea, taking turns to anchor near the loading island, but not too close, because strong winds rose suddenly in those parts and the ship could be smashed on the rocks.

William Hughes photographed during a shore-leave in Australia.

We then had two shifts working (the sailors did all the work as there were no dockers). One boat sailed under the chute, which ran from the spot the Chileans were working to overhang the sea. The sailors had to keep the tender steady under this chute, and took turns in pairs to hold the bags whilst the Guano came down all over us. We had covered ourselves as well as we could with sacks or canvas. Boots were ruined in days, so we wrapped our feet in sacks. It was really filthy, nasty, evil-smelling stuff, but farmers wanted it and paid well for it. I read somewhere of an Anglesey farmer paying over £300 annually for guano. A great deal of money in those days.

When loaded, the boat was rowed to the ship and unloaded by the other half of the crew, using a winch to lift the bags and then stowed them in the hold. Not a pleasant cargo, but very profitable, much better than ballast. Conditions at the Guano Islands were bad, even dreadful. When ashore there was little or nothing to do in the primitive townships. Wherever you were, it was hot and humid, the air was pungent and there were thousands of flies around, including mosquitoes. Sometimes ships were moored here for months at a time.

This first voyage on the *Beeswing* lasted over two years. We called at Valpariso, Antofagasta and Iquique for short periods, then sailed to Callita Calloso and stayed there without once going ashore for six months! The price of guano had dropped in the world market so we had to wait to get a better return.

We then sailed back to Newcastle, Australia, but calling this time at Pitcairn Island, arriving at dawn on Christmas Eve 1906, and were met by dozens of islanders (descendants of the mutineers of the *Bounty*) expert boatmen, their boats loaded with fruit of all kinds, not to give away, but to sell, and sell at rather steep prices too. We shared a great deal with them, meat, food, clothes, etc. As they left us they sang a tune very much like the one sung at the Eisteddfod when the exiles return. Fletcher Christian's family were still there and they were very proud of him.

From Pitcairn we sailed back to Newcastle, but there was a strike on again and we were there for two months, however we had a great time. There were many Welsh people inviting us to their homes and wishing to have news of what was going on at home. Very welcoming, and speaking Welsh!

From Newcastle we had a load for Coquimbo and there had to load tatal nitrate for Rotterdam. Round the Horn again but this time we had decent weather, although there were many icebergs around, it was clear, so we were able to clear the point of the Horn in two days. I was paid off at Rotterdam but, as I wanted to get my certificate, I went to King Edward VII's Nautical School in London instead of going home, although I'd been away over two years.

The *Deccan*

In February 1907, I'd passed my certificate so I went home to Porthmadog and took three weeks' holiday. I was offered and accepted a post as second mate on a full-rigged ship called the *Deccan* loading at Cardiff with coal and cargo for Callita Colloso.

The Deccan.

We had a very bad storm in the Bay of Biscay, but nothing compared with what was to come at the Horn. This time it took us almost eight weeks to get round, with constant high seas and winds. We were tied to safety lines all the time on deck and two men were tied at the wheel. But first let me tell you something that happened before we actually reached the Horn.

One day, I was off watch when I heard some activity and shouting. We had come across a dismasted ship with just one small sail showing. It was the *Dyonome*, with a distress signal showing. We signalled them (of course they were hand-signals with flags in those days, and it was very difficult to send and read in rough weather). We asked them if they wanted to be taken off, and, as I was the one to take the boat, I got it ready whilst waiting for their reply. After more than half-an-hour we managed to read their reply, which was, 'No, we could not face the Horn again, thank you. We shall try to reach Montevideo'. I was very pleased, as I don't think we would have come back from that rescue attempt. That very night our main boat was smashed by huge waves. Over

40 years later, I read in *Sea Breezes* that the *Dyonome* had actually made it to Montevideo and eventually got home safely. The story, told by the brother of the carpenter on board, told how we had come to help. But when our offer meant taking them off the *Dyonome* and sailing back round the Horn, the Captain said, 'No'.

We got round the Horn, thanks to the skill and bravery of Captain Rees, whose father, incidentally, was Baptist minister of Bethel, Holyhead, and is buried in the chapel cemetery. His brother was General (Dagger) Rees, the famous soldier who was in Burma with General Wingate and the Chindits during the Second World War.

At Callita Calloso, we discharged the coal and sailed a further 100 miles to Callito Bono to load nitrate. There were no wharves at Callita Bono so we anchored in the bay and loaded the nitrate in bags from tenders. We were three parts loaded when the *Marion Fraser* came and anchored near us. The *Marion Fraser* belonged to our company and there were many friends aboard, so we were brought up to date with news of home, etc. There was also a director of the company on board and he asked Captain Rees to transfer to the *Marian Fraser* for the homeward voyage.

I should have told you another story about Captain Rees. He had been captain of the *Morven* and had sailed to Australia and on to San Francisco with his fiancée — a New Zealander — on board, intending to marry in Holyhead, with his father officiating. However, they both fell in love with San Francisco and decided to marry there. They were in the Honeymoon Suite of a hotel there when the earthquake of 1906 started. They managed to escape to the ship and saw the fires and the city collapsing from the relative safety of the boat.

On their homeward voyage they were due to discharge at Limerick but a heavy gale drove them ashore on Loop Head Creek and the *Morven* was wrecked. Mrs Rees was taken ashore by boat, but the captain and most of the crew climbed ashore over the bowsprit.

The *Marion Fraser*

Captain Rees moved from the *Deccan* to the *Marion Fraser* and he invited me to join him as second mate. We were to round the Horn to Melbourne and up to Antafagasta and Callita Calloso. After loading nitrate there, we were to sail for home. On the outward journey we had very unusual weather at the Horn and were almost becalmed. In fact, it was perhaps the most dangerous of all crossings for me. There was no wind at all and we were drifting nearer and nearer the rocks. All the boats had been loaded with essentials — food, water, spare clothes, blankets, flares, etc., and we had almost reached the shore when a slight breeze caught the sail and we were spared.

On the return journey, however, the Horn was back to its usual self. It was all hands on duty for most of the days until we were clear. Most of the crew were asleep when the wind started blowing again. Captain Rees did not want to disturb the resting crew so he asked me, 'Do you think you could reef the sails without calling the crew?'

The Marion Fraser.

'Yes,' I said, and after a couple of hours the sails were safe and I joined him on the poop deck.

'Tired Mr Hughes? You're only a little fellow but you're worth your weight in gold!'

Another thing I should tell you about sailing on long voyages was that the captain or the officers had to act as doctors or sometimes dentists. I myself set a broken shoulder and broken arms and legs. I also recall a Finnish sailor who became very ill with some fever. The captain had given him some pills to try to cool him and had set a young sailor to sit outside the cabin and look in now and then to give him a cold drink. But we were all involved furling the sails some time later, when someone spotted him high in the rigging. Before anyone could do anything about it, he fell on to the deck and was killed instantly.

As always, all the crew attended the burial service. The body was stitched in canvas with some irons and a hole left for water to enter. I say that, because I recall the very first time I had to sew a body canvas I forgot the hole. It was totally waterproof and the body followed the ship for hours on end.

Another ritual was the sale of the dead man's possessions. None of us carried valuables, but had essentials and perhaps something we had bought as a present. The captain or the first officer would carefully list all the dead man's belongings, remove whatever he considered the family would wish to have, and then hold an auction of the rest of his belongings. It was unbelievable what the sailors would pay out of their small, hard-earned wages, in order to help the dead man's family. The details of his death, cause of death, what medication he had received, together with a list of his belongings, money, and the details of the sale were sent to the owners, to be despatched to the bereaved family.

To return to the *Marion Fraser*. We sailed from Mexalonis round the Horn and reached the Equator in 47 days, an excellent run, and in fact, with full sail we passed the steamer *Minnehaha* in the Atlantic and reached Dover, where we had a tug to take us on to

Hamburg. I had been away over two years and my family had meanwhile moved to live to Liverpool because all the men in the family now sailed to and from that port, and Porthmadog was in decline. After leave, I joined the *Beeswing* as first mate with my youngest brother, Arthur, as cabin boy. We sailed from Cardiff to Antofagasta in Chile. Again, we had heavy weather at the Horn and it took almost five weeks to cross.

The second mate broke his shoulder blade and I, being the last to attend a First Aid course, had to set it. The doctor at Antofagasta said I had done a very good job. From Antofagasta in Chile we went to Newcastle, Australia, for coal for Valpariso and on to Mexalonis, where we loaded nitrate for Dunkirk — again, as ever, the crew loading. The voyage home was long, and the ship was in dire need of cleaning and refurbishing. Arthur had studied hard and the captain had spent hours helping him. He was a good pupil and passed as second and first mate in no time. Aged 34, he passed his master's ticket.

I went back to the Nautical School and passed my Square-Rigged Master's Certificate. At this stage I was in two minds whether to go into steam or stick to sail. I had been offered the captaincy of the *Beeswing*. It was to take a full load of copper ore to Mexalonis. I had to consider my future. The ship was getting older and needed refurbishing. It had also been up for sale — in fact some potential buyers came to look it over when I was left in charge of it at Rotterdam following the last trip. The cargo was heavy and dirty, and if there were trouble, it would not help my career. So, after a sleepless night, I regretfully refused the command and decided to try steam. That was to be the end of my time in sailing ships. I knew that although I had my certificate as master I would have to start in steam as third officer. I also knew that the days of sailing ships were numbered.

Sail or steam?

I joined the steamer *Ben Rath* as third mate sailing from Cardiff, carrying coal to the Black Sea and returning with grain for Rotterdam and Swansea. I left the *Ben Rath* after only one voyage, as I did not like her at all. In fact I had some difficulty leaving her, as they did not send a replacement until I stated in front of witnesses that I would leave at Cardiff whether or not there was a replacement.

My next berth was with the Booth Line, sailing on the *Lanfranc* from Cherbourg, calling at Lisbon, Madeira, Para then 1,000 miles up the Amazon to Manaus. It was a most interesting voyage. We carried cargo and could accommodate passengers. The current up the Amazon was around five knots and in parts it was so wide that you seemed to be in a huge lake. When you neared the bank you could see the forest with huge trees almost intertwined many feet above and a variety of animals and fish to be seen, especially crocodiles. From the point where the river Negro joins the Amazon, there are two colours in the water. The Amazon itself is brown with silt, whilst the Negro is fresh from the mountains and is blue/green in colour. This continues all the way to the Atlantic Ocean and the water tastes fresh for many miles into the salty sea.

It took almost two weeks to unload and reload with rubber, nuts and some timber. The passengers went off on various tours. The *Lanfranc* could accommodate up to 200 passengers and there were all kinds of activities arranged for them when at sea. On the return voyage we started stopping at Fishguard for passengers to catch a train to London, but that venture didn't last long.

One event whilst on the *Lanfranc* is worth relating. It was 14 April 1912 and I was down below off watch when Captain Kenthorne called me to the bridge. As I got there he said, 'It would be a shame for you to miss this sight Mr Hughes'. Approaching us was a huge four-funnelled passenger ship with all lights blazing. It was the *Titanic* on her maiden voyage, having sailed from Queenstown (Cork), its last port of call. Captain Kenthorne sent her a signal

CAPTAIN WILLIAM HENRY HUGHES, DSC

wishing, 'God Speed', which was acknowledged by Captain Smith. When we reached Liverpool, we heard the tragic news. We may well have been the last people to see the famous ship.

More tales

Another story I should have related concerns my two brothers, Jesse and Oswald. In fact, I shall tell you two or three stories about them. The first takes us back many years to the time when Jesse joined my father on the *Nesta* and I had to leave her for the *Cambria*. Jesse hated cooking, or rather the preparation of food — cleaning cabbages, peeling potatoes and the like was not for sailors — but that was the pattern. The last to join a ship became ordinary seaman/cook. Because Jesse disliked the job, others teased him, particularly his Uncle Will Hope. Jesse had an idea.

They were sailing from Caernarfon for Cadiz and had crossed the bar and sailing in a good wind for Bardsey when Jesse reported to his father that he had found a stowaway. Captain Harry was astounded and asked who on earth would want to come with them. Jesse said it was his brother Oswald and almost in the same breath said, 'Does that mean that he now becomes cook and I am a proper sailor?' He was told to fetch Oswald and both of them were reprimanded and put to work. The ship put in to Swansea and Oswald was sent home, care of the guard on the train, to go back to school in shame, having been absent for three weeks.

My brother Jesse had sailed with me on the *Marion Fraser*. I was mate and Jesse an able seaman. Just past the Falklands we had terrible weather. The ship was full of water and we had to use safety lines. One day it was so bad the captain did something I had never seen before, or since. He poured oil through the scuppers to calm the waters whilst the crew went below to try to right the cargo, which had shifted badly. It took most of the night and the captain ordered a tot of rum to be issued. I was ordered to supervise and the men queued up to receive it — among them was my little brother, Jesse, who held his mug out. I told him to go to

*William's brother, Jesse Hughes,
photographed when a captain serving
on the Holyhead ferries.
[Lady Jean of Penrhos]*

the galley for cocoa. It was only then that the crew knew we were brothers, although there were many Welsh speakers on board. I did not want them to think Jesse would get favours from me.

Before I set off on my last voyage in sail on the *Beeswing*, I had gone to Liverpool docks to see my brothers, Jesse and Oswald, setting off on the *Milverton*. They were sailing to Cardiff to load coal for Calleo. I sailed about three weeks later on the *Beeswing* for Newcastle, Australia. When I got to Newcastle, I enquired about the *Milverton* and was told that its cargo of coal had caught fire and they had to sail to Rio de Janeiro. There they doused the fire and emptied the cargo to cool it, then sailed on to Newcastle and Calleo. I enquired about Jesse and Oswald but was told there was only one Hughes on the *Milverton* leaving Newcastle. They had no record of crew arrivals. I was very concerned and wondered which brother was missing, and why.

When we got to Calleo, there were dozens of ships there as usual. The captain made enquiries and found that the *Milverton* was further north and, as he knew I was concerned about my brothers, he had arranged with the agent, who was going there the following morning, to take me with him. Sure enough, an open boat with a lugsail and oars came for me in the morning. The agent was a swarthy Italian speaking little English. There was quite a swell, but we rowed well. I had not brought any food with me, not realising how far away the *Milverton* was, but I'd had a good breakfast. He had a little charcoal stove and slices of meat, which he offered to share with me. I honestly couldn't fancy it, his hands were filthy and the meat didn't look very fresh. There were 30 miles more rowing and sailing to go and by 9 p.m. I was starving, and would have eaten the stove. The meat tasted wonderful.

It was 2 a.m. when eventually we found the *Milverton* and the watchman directed me to a cabin and there I found Jesse, fast asleep. He stirred and looked at me then turned over as if to sleep, then looked at me again in the low lamplight and said calmly, 'Oh, its you.' I immediately asked about Oswald, as I was afraid that he would have been injured, or worse, in the fire. 'Oh,' he said, 'He jumped ship in Newcastle, Australia, and got a job as foreman in a ginger beer factory.'

I said, 'You were in charge of him, what will Mother say?' He replied , 'I did go after him before we sailed, but he was going to save some money in the factory to buy clothes, food and equipment to go prospecting for gold, I could not have done more.' I agreed with him.

The Milverton. *[GAS XS/1279/7/50e]*

I slept on board the *Milverton* until morning and got a lift on a boat to the port of Ancona, where I was eventually picked up by a boat from the *Beeswing*.

Oswald went prospecting with some others, but failed miserably to get any gold. He returned to the ginger beer factory and got his foreman job back. He saved his money and eventually returned to Liverpool on a foreign ship.

Earlier I mentioned Will Hope, our uncle. He was a wonderful sailor and a boxer of some repute, but when ashore he liked his drink and got into all kinds of scrapes. He teased my brother Jesse mercilessly, particularly when Jesse was the cook. My father had trouble persuading Jesse to join the crew if Will Hope and his bosom pal 'Compo' had signed on.

I remember on one occasion they were sailing from Hull and were living in Liverpool. Jesse was told to find a carriage whilst father saw to the rest of the crew. When it came near the time to leave, Jesse leaned out of the window and saw his father with the guard locking one of the non-corridor carriages. When he came back Jesse asked him what he'd been doing. 'Oh just making sure my crew will get to Hull,' he said. The crew turned out to be Will Hope and Compo, both very drunk. When they got to Hull they were still fast asleep with their bowler hats tightly pulled down on their heads.

Jesse had his own back on another occasion. They were at some small South American port and Will Hope and Compo failed to return to the ship one night. In the morning Jesse was sent to town to get fresh meat, fruit and vegetables. His father told him to look out for the missing pair. As he got into the town he saw the police with the 'chain gang' of people who had broken the rules the night before and were paying for their misdeeds by cleaning latrines, etc. Then he heard a 'duet' calling him 'Jesse tell your father to come quickly to bail us out, this is awful'. When he got back on board Jesse took his time before telling his father, who smiled and said, 'I think we'll teach them a lesson and fetch them just before we sail on the evening tide.'

Once on the *Marion Fraser* I had become friendly with a German sailor named Fritz, a huge, powerful fellow, very pleasant and with good English, which he had picked up in Porthmadog. We had been moored for some time off the Guano islands when another ship moored about half-a-mile away. We both knew some of her crew, so he suggested we go across that evening for a chat. We were not allowed to use the ship's boat, so it meant swimming. We were both strong swimmers so we waited for darkness and then swam across.

It was almost ten o'clock when we started back on a lovely calm night. We were nearing our ship when we ran into a shoal of small seals followed by some porpoises. I could feel them against me and was almost being lifted out of the water by the porpoises. I continued swimming and soon reached the gangway but there was no sign of Fritz. I looked around and saw something white in the distance so I swam towards it. It was Fritz and he was perfectly still as though in a coma. I grabbed his arm and called his name. Suddenly he seemed to wake from a trance and swam at top speed for the ship. When I joined him he said he had never experienced anything like that before. He had obviously had a panic attack and seemed to freeze in the water. He was very shaken.

Cape Horn and the Southern Ocean was the biggest test for all sailing ships and sailors. Some years were worse than others according to Commander Alan Villiers. In his book called *The Battle with The Horn* he wrote, 'Between 50 degrees south, east and west of the Horn was the test and you had to keep well off the land and the wind was almost always against you. At the same time you had snow and ice. All sails were changed for heavy weather and safety lines were set up to save lives. Even with these, there were dreadful accidents and strong men were thrown and almost pulped against the hull by the sea. As for changing the rigging during this weather, it was almost impossible. I have seen heavy weather sails torn to shreds in minutes. Two men were strapped to the wheel on occasions like this.'

I remember on one outward voyage we had a dreadful storm in

the Bay of Biscay and the wheel was wrenched from the sailor's hands and it spun until it smashed to pieces. They rigged the donkey engine to get steam and eventually got wires attached to the rudder so that we could keep some control of the ship. Meanwhile it was being thrown around like a top. When eventually we got control and could steer a straight course, the carpenter set about making a new wheel. He and a Danish sailor took the iron cap off the top of the main mast as a hub and the carpenter made spokes for a temporary wheel. This served us all the way round the Horn and we had a reasonable passage. We had passed the Horn and were sailing north when someone recalled that the *Harlech Castle* had been wrecked at a point near where we were sailing. A boat was launched, and in no time returned with the wheel, which was later fitted to our ship for the return journey.

On the small Porthmadog ships we could get fresh food every few days and I always found it wholesome and plentiful. My father did most of the cooking, but I cooked quite a lot too. On the *Faith* I cooked all the meals for eight people and never had a complaint. On the larger ships the cooks worked harder than anyone because they had to see to the breakfast and all the meals through to supper and often worked until after nine at night. The cook was responsible for his own fires and even had to clean the chimneys He chose his time and pulled a chain up and down the chimney setting sparks everywhere. He was often called out to help the sailors as well. As it was the only fire aboard, wet clothes would be hanging around everywhere to dry. I recall someone complaining that one of his socks had been stolen. It was discovered in the last ladleful from the stockpot!

On the larger ships, you stored food for a long journey and you had no refrigeration in those days. We used to paint all the potatoes with whitewash to seal them. Before use they were soaked in water and then peeled,

Bread was a problem because the allowances were set down by law, so much for each person per day. Weevils used to get into the bread tanks and used to appear like caraway seed in the loaf. When preparing for a voyage, an important task was to clean out the flour bins.

Once on the *Beeswing* it almost cost me my life. They had used the candles to fumigate the four flour bins that were in the lazereet. The sailor doing the job was too fat to get into the bin to clean it out properly; nor could the second mate get in, so I was asked to do it. I had cleaned three out of the four, but felt rather odd and disliked the smell. Fortunately, someone called for me and as I did not answer, they looked into the bins and found me unconscious. They had a great deal of trouble getting me out and all the time I was getting more and more of the gas. Thankfully I eventually came to. Since then, they have had to use a wind sail to direct air into bins when cleaning them.

For the first few days of a voyage you had plenty of fresh meat, steak, etc Some ships had hens, or even a pig on board but, after the fresh meat finished, we had salt bacon or corned beef. We had fresh eggs for a few days and if we had hens there were eggs all the way. My brother Jesse was not so fortunate on one ship, a sister ship to the *Milverton*. Food was bad and in short supply. I liked his description of her. 'One long voyage on her and you could wipe your nose with the skin of your tummy.'

As second mate on the *Marion Frazer* I was in charge of the paraffin and had to ensure that all the lamps, including navigation lights, were topped up. I also had to blow the cabin lights out at night. Not always a popular job if the sailor had a good book.

On the homeward bound journey we made the ship as smart as possible. The decks were washed then scrubbed down with a soft stone, which we called Hallistone; it brought up the original colour of the wood. Sometimes, we put a lick of paint here and there on the hull. You can imagine that after months, sometimes years at sea, the ship would be showing signs of wear and tear.

In the early years I sailed mostly with my father and learnt a great deal from him but when I went deep sea there were long periods when we did not see each other. I recall one period of five years when we did not see each other once. He was very kind and yet very tough and hard and an excellent sailor. He could smell or sense bad weather and seemed always prepared for the elements. I, and my brothers, learnt a great deal from him. He was not used to children although he was the father of eight. Here are a few tales about him.

My brother Jesse had adopted two ducks. He fed them regularly and they followed him to and from the sea to a box he had at the back of the house. Father arrived home one Christmas Eve and told mother that he would see to the Christmas dinner. He was a good cook and the table was loaded. The last thing brought in was a huge plate with two cooked ducks on it. Jesse then came in and said he had searched everywhere but couldn't find his ducks. Everybody refused to eat the roast duck except father. Jesse was heartbroken.

I had a pet dog called Jack that I thought the world of. We were sailing to Spain where quarantine laws are very strict, although I was not aware of this when I smuggled Jack aboard. Jack soon made his presence known and I received the worst telling off I ever had. I never saw Jack again. Later I was told that father put Jack in a potato sack with a huge lump of coal and dropped him overboard. When he saw my tears he said, 'Why are you crying? I didn't throw Jesse into the sea, it was only a dog.'

My father's eldest sister, aunt Jane, was married and lived with her family at Pencei, a large house right on the docks. One of them, my cousin Dilys Melinda, a lovely little girl, died at the age of six, and I recall her funeral. After the funeral they brought out her possessions, including her little purse full of money. Aunt Jane decided to share the money between her friends who were at the funeral and we had 10*d*. each. I was anxious to spend some of this fortune and went to Ann Grace's shop for a halfpenny worth of sweets, and that is how I spent it all, in halfpennies at Ann Grace's shop in Porthmadog.

Father was quite fearless; I sailed with him for years in all kinds of weather and saw him dealing with all kinds of difficult and dangerous situations, in nature and with people, ashore and within his crew, yet strangely, he never learnt to swim. I wonder sometimes if he was afraid of water.

I was told that when he went to a South American port with the *Edward Seymour* the local agent told him that a white captain, who had contracted yellow fever, had been left to die in a hut outside the village. Father got some food and water and went to find the wretched man. When they were about to sail, he went back to the hut, lifted the man over his shoulder and carried him back to the *Edward Seymour* to a bed he had put on the stern. He died the following day, but was given a 'Christian burial' at sea. The crew, who were rather scared, were told to keep themselves clean and take plenty of fresh air. Father was the only one to handle him and he suffered no ill effects.

My mother was a lovely woman, in looks and nature. She was also very strong in spirit. When you consider that she brought up eight children on her own more or less, you will appreciate that. There is one story about Jesse that shows her true spirit. Jesse got into conversation with some visitors on the beach in Borth-y-gest who asked if there was anyone who could take them out in a boat. He knew of a good boat lying idle nearby, he could borrow it and it would be back before the owner returned from work.

So off they set with the 11-year old feeling very grown up. Unfortunately there were tides and river currents of which he was not aware. Suddenly he realised that no amount of rowing could get him back ashore and they eventually landed on the opposite shore near Talsarnau. The visitors were pleased to get ashore anywhere. Jesse set off on a long walk back. When he got back home he confessed to his mother what he'd done.

Early next morning they set off to walk to Talsarnau. When they got there they got into the boat and rowed back to Borth-y-gest with mother doing most of the rowing. More was to come. When the owner came home that evening, she stood behind Jesse whilst he admitted what he had done and apologised to the man. He never borrowed anyone else's boat again. Nor did she ever mention the incident again.

The final move — steam

On leaving the *Lanfranc* on the regular run to Manaus, 1,000 miles up the Amazon, I got a post as third officer on the *Canning* (Lampert & Holt), sailing on a regular run from Manchester to New York. This meant that I was able to see my family in Liverpool more often. Each round trip took about three weeks. I stayed with this firm and enjoyed it until August 1914 when I obtained a post as second officer on the LNWR cross-channel services, sailing from Holyhead to Ireland. Again you had to start at the lower end, no matter what experience or qualifications you had. You also had to start in the cargo boats and wait for a vacancy in the passenger boats before you got promotion.

The London & North Western Railway
Steamship Company (LNWR) — war

When I first joined the LNWR boats in August 1914, they had four what they called 'express boats', namely: the *Cambria* (built by William Denny, 1897), *Hibernia* (William Denny, 1900), *Anglia* (William Denny, 1900) and the *Scotia* (William Denny, 1902). Two of these were almost immediately requisitioned by the Royal Navy — the *Hibernia* (renamed HMS *Tara*, as they already had an HMS *Hibernia*) and the *Scotia*; both were sent to the Mediterranean and Red Sea. The *Cambria* and the *Anglia* were sent down south for trooping to France.

The *Anglia* later became a hospital ship — but was sunk by a mine in the English Channel. The *Hibernia* (HMS *Tara*) was torpedoed by a submarine in the Mediterranean in 1915 and the crew were to suffer greatly in the North African desert at the hands of Senussi tribesmen, until they were rescued by a car patrol led by the Duke of Westminster. The *Scotia* was also bombed at Dunkirk and badly damaged. My brother Jesse was serving on her at the time. She was repaired at Dunkirk before returning to Holyhead. Later she and the *Cambria* were renamed *Arvonia* and *Menevia*. This was to preserve the names *Cambria*, *Hibernia*, *Scotia*, and *Anglia* for the new ships ordered as replacements from William Denny.

There were also three ships running to Greenore named *Rathmore*, *Galtee More* and *Greenore*. The latter was found to be unsuitable for that port and was transferred to the Dublin run, as were the other two some time later, leaving the stand-by boats *Connemara* and *Rostrevor* to do the Greenore run. On 3 November1916 the *Connemara* was lost with all hands on the bar just after leaving for Holyhead. This followed a collision with a coaster named the *Retriever*, which was sailing from Garston. Altogether, over ninety lives were lost on that fatal night. Most of the crew were from Holyhead and the whole town was in mourning.

Although it was a clear but stormy night, it seems that they simply did not see each other. Both vessels sank immediately with one man from the *Retriever* as the only survivor. He had managed to swim ashore. The keepers at the Haulbowline Lighthouse, only a quarter-of-a-mile away were unable to summon help and it was only when a local farmer went to his fields and the foreshore in the morning and found them covered with bodies and dead cattle, that the alarm was raised. The *Connemara* was upside down a few hundred yards from the shore with the *Retriever* nearby.

The master of the *Galtee More*, on the first trip out from Holyhead had seen the wreck, but thought it was a stranded submarine rather than the keel of the *Connemara*, nor did he know that the *Connemara* had not arrived in Holyhead from the previous voyage.

There were seven cargo boats in Holyhead; *Slieve More*, *Slieve Bawn*, *Slieve Bloom*, *Slieve Gallion*, *Slieve Donard*, *Snowdon* and *South Stack*. One was converted to run to the Isle of Man, but that did not last long. I was appointed to the *Snowdon*, but you were liable to be moved to any other ship.

The Royal Mail contract at this time was held by the City of

Dublin Company, as it had been since 1851. In 1914 they had four mail boats running from the mail pier. They were the *Connaught, Leinster, Ulster* and *Munster*. There was a small train running from the mail pier to the station, where passengers transferred to the main line. During the First World War they lost two of their ships, the *Connaught* was torpedoed whilst on war service in the English Channel, and in 1918 and the *Leinster* was sunk by enemy action in the Irish Sea, a month before the end of the war, with great loss of life. Again there were many Holyheadians in the crew, and as passengers on that fatal night. This town suffered greatly during the First World War.

My first post was as third officer on the *Snowdon* a cargo boat sailing from Holyhead to Dublin. The cargo was mainly cattle and horses. When on certain duties you were obliged to walk down the central gangway to ensure that all the animals were all right. There were cowmen and ostlers of course but the company insisted on 'the officer of the watch' checking on the animals, especially in rough weather. Horses in particular went rather wild; they snapped and salivated as you walked, or crept, past checking for broken legs or other injuries. I disliked that part of my duty intensely and almost crawled along the gangway. I could almost feel them snapping at the back of my collar.

As soon as we docked of course they were handed over to the shore gang and eventually to the owners who either sent them onwards by rail or road or to pens or stables, or even fields on the outskirts of town such as Cae Bogue, Kingsland. Mr Bogue had been a well-known cattle dealer in Holyhead.

Many valuable racehorses were carried in the cargo boats for race meetings in this country. They had their own grooms to look after them and no one else was allowed to touch them. There were regular animal sales held on the other side and we had many dealers and farmers Irish, English and Welsh who travelled regularly to buy or sell stock.

During the period from 1914 to 1920 I served on several different ships to various destinations. There were usually three crews for the regular sailings in order to keep up to the schedules. You could be called at short notice to take over in another ship to Dublin, Kingstown or Greenore. I served for some time on the *Rostrevor* sailing to Greenore. It was a rather awkward harbour with a four to six-knot current, but it made life interesting. For some time I was second officer to Captain Copeland, which I recall as being among my happiest periods at sea.

Man overboard!

It was on the *Rostrevor* that I had the first exciting event with the LNWR service on the Irish Sea. We were reversing out of Greenore. I had been overseeing the stern crew on the moorings and was returning to the bridge when I heard some shouting. As I reached the bridge the captain signalled for the ship to move back to the pier. The first officer shouted that the carpenter had fallen overboard as he tried to close the gangway door. As we came level with the pier I jumped ashore and took off my coat and shoes. I could see Mr Pritchard (the carpenter) trying to swim against the current, so I dived in and soon reached him. He was totally exhausted, so I got hold of his collar, turned him over and we

SS Rostrevor.

The gold watch presented to William Hughes by the ship's company of the RMS Rostrevor.

drifted with the tide. In no time the ship's boat came along and picked us up and took us back to the pier. There he was given artificial respiration and he revived. Within an hour-and-a-half, the *Rosstrevor*, with Mr Pritchard on board, had sailed for Holyhead.

Sometime later, there was a ceremony at the Marine Superintendent's Office when I was awarded a gold watch inscribed thus: 'Presented to Mr W. H. Hughes by the ship's company of RMS *Rostrevor* in recognition of his bravery on 25 July 1919', together with a handsome cheque from the company. Mr Pritchard continued to serve the company for many years before retiring. He lived in Station Street, Holyhead.

In 1921, the Irish Mail contract, valued at £100,000 was awarded to the LNWR Shipping Company. As I mentioned earlier, the Dublin Packet Steamship Company had held the contract since 1851. With two of their four ships lost during the war, and the remaining two getting old and in need of replacement, it was almost a foregone conclusion. Since the beginning, the LNWR ships had run from the station. Passengers had only a few yards to walk from ship to train (or train to ship). On the same site was the excellent Railway Hotel where they could eat or sleep in comfort. There were plenty of porters and stewards available to see to their every need.

The City of Dublin Steam Packet Company went out of business and the two remaining ships; the *Ulster* and the *Munster* were sold to the Germans for scrap. The LNWR company was obliged to take on the officers and, as I recall, we took on one captain, two chief officers and three or four second officers. This meant another slow down in promotion.

Four new ships arrived from William Denny in 1920 and 1921 bearing the same names *Anglia, Hibernia, Cambria*, and *Scotia*. The Holyhead inner harbour had been deepened to 21 feet all over (previously 17 ft one side only), so there was no difficulty in navigating in or out. The cargo sheds were on the town side and were ideal for loading and unloading with goods, etc on the other side of the sheds. Unfortunately, the troubles in Ireland were flaring up and the papers were full of reports of deaths. Politicians were travelling backwards and forwards to try and agree a satisfactory compromise. Understandably our crews were reluctant to spend much time ashore during this period.

Arvonia and trouble

I was second officer on the *Arvonia* and we had been on loan to the Irish Free State Government. The orders came for us to proceed to Dublin. We had been there for ten days when a battalion of Free State troops boarded and we took them to Limerick, as it was too dangerous for them to travel overland. A short time later we had another full load of Free State troops and this time accompanied by three generals; Emmet, Tobin and Richards. We sailed under sealed orders that were to be opened after sailing.

The orders stated that we were to proceed to Cork and unload the troops but, when the pilot came aboard at Cobh and saw the Free State troops, he became quite agitated and refused to lead us. He said that the rebels had sunk vessels and other obstacles in our path. It was about 4 a.m. with dawn breaking on a lovely June morning. The generals put pressure on the pilot to do his duty, but he absolutely refused.

Visibility was good, but we had to take note of the pilot's warning, so we were moving very slowly checking for obstacles and looking for a landing. Ahead we could see a couple of wooden

The TSS Hibernia *(left) and* Cambria, *berthed at Holyhead.*
[Maritime Museum, Holyhead]

The TSS Hibernia *in 1930. [Maritime Museum, Holyhead]*

dolphins at a small shipyard called Passage West. As we got near we could see that there was a plank about 16 feet long to get you ashore from the dolphin. The difficulty was to get the *Arvonia* moored, as there was no one ashore to take and secure our mooring ropes.

It was then that the firing started from the sheds about 100 yards away and above us. It was heavy rifle fire and it was hitting our bridge and funnel on the port side. On such a calm quiet morning it sounded particularly loud. Our Free State troops were under orders not to return the fire. As the ship was sheering about without any speed, Captain Roberts was anxious to get her tied up. I decided to try to get ashore using the plank. I waited for a lull in the firing, then jumped on the dolphin and was just getting the plank in place, when they opened up again with bullets flying everywhere. I managed to get ashore and rolled under the nearest shed where it was safe. I signalled to a soldier aboard to be ready with the rope, and waited for another lull in the firing then sped over the plank for the rope. As I reached the top of the plank again, they spotted me and restarted firing. I managed to get the rope over the bollard and dashed back on to the ship safely. I was met by Captain Roberts who said, 'You lead a charmed life Mr Hughes, I did not expect to see you alive again and here you are uninjured.' The three generals also shook my hand and thanked me.

By now permission had come through for the Free State troops to return the fire and to clear the rebels so that the ship could continue to Cork. They did this, but not without casualties on both sides. The ship's lounge became a first aid station, as well as a church, where a local priest carried out the Last Rites. Altogether, we were there for four days and the ship was quite badly damaged on the port side.

Eventually we sailed slowly up to Cork to unload, but even there we were subjected to some intermittent sniper fire. As soon as we unloaded we sailed back to Dublin, and thence to Holyhead. On the recommendation of Captain Roberts and the Marine

Superintendent of the LMS Railway (which we had now become), I was presented with a handsome cheque, together with a silver cigarette case inscribed 'To 2nd Officer W. H. Hughes for conspicuous bravery and devotion to duty.'

The SS *Alexandra*

About three weeks later I was serving as second officer on RMS *Anglia* under Captain J. E. Telfer, and was on duty in Dublin Docks when, at around 11.30 p.m., an officer and some Irish Free State troops came aboard and requested Captain Telfer to launch a boat and convey them to the Irish Lights Vessel, SS *Alexandra*, moored in the harbour, the said vessel having been raided by the irregulars and left with sea cocks open. The captain immediately ordered me to take a boat and ten men to do whatever we could to save this important vessel.

When we got to the *Alexandra* she was settling in the water and we could hear the sound of water below. When we got down to the engine room the water was up to our knees. There was no light except for my torch and a hand lamp from the boat. We searched in vain for tools in order to close the seacocks. Meanwhile I had some of the firemen try to raise steam in order to get the pumps working. We tried everything to try and stem the flow, which was very strong, and eventually slowed it down with heavy mats with Mr Doughty sitting on them. Later, the chief engineer of the *Alexandra* returned, having been released by the irregulars (thinking that the ship would have sunk by then). He was able to find tools to close the valves properly and by then the pumps were doing their work, so we returned to the *Anglia* at 2.15 a.m. and reported to Captain Telfer.

Almost twelve months later, on 25 August 1923, the Commissioners of the Irish Lights sent a sum of money as 'a token of thanks for saving the Irish Light Ship *Alexandra*'. I was given £5, and each of the 10 men with me were given £2 each, a total of £25.

The *Anglia*, one of four new ships built by Denny in 1920/1, had a short, active life. It was mostly held as a reserve ship in Holyhead and had an active life of about two years. In 1924 it was withdrawn and sent to Barrow and eventually to Troon for scrap in 1935. She must have cost around a quarter of a million pounds yet was sold for £18,000. A few years earlier, a Canadian firm had offered £150,000 for her but she was on 'Stand By'. However the three other ships were adequate and reliable for the service at Holyhead and the 'Stand By' was hardly ever used.

Another rescue

It was a busy run with plenty to do during the three-and-a-half hour crossing, although people often asked if I got bored on the short crossing compared with the long voyages on sailing ships, or steaming up the Amazon. There was always something to do, even though we didn't have to worry about sails or a change in the wind. There was always the unexpected happening. For example, I was transferred to the *Cambria* and a short time after joining her, I was on duty one night in Dublin harbour when a lady jumped overboard — trying to commit suicide. I took off my shoes, overcoat and jacket and dived in. In no time I came up to her and held her until a boat came. Later I received a Royal Humane Society Testimonial on Vellum for saving life. She had changed her mind as soon as she touched the water.

On another occasion, I was second officer with Captain O'Neill on the RMS *Scotia* and we were about half-way across to Holyhead. I was doing my rounds on a nasty night and had been to the first class lounge, and was checking the third class, when I noticed a man whom I'd seen earlier in the first class lounge. This was unusual, but there was no rule against it, as there was the other way around — no one with a third class ticket would be allowed into the first class lounge. I spoke to the steward and advised him to keep an eye on the gentleman as he seemed rather disturbed, and I continued my duties.

I had returned to the bridge and taken over from Captain O'Neill

TSS Scotia *entering Holyhead harbour.*

some twenty minutes or so, when the shout 'Man Overboard!' was heard. I sensed immediately that it was the same man. I threw two lifebelts overboard; one lighted, and gave orders to turn back on our original course. The *Scotia* had been doing 21 knots at the time. As we turned, Captain O'Neill arrived on the bridge but asked me to continue, as he had not yet got used to the light.

When we got to the spot where I estimated the man had gone over, I stopped engines and launched a boat setting off in the direction I thought he might be, but it seemed like a forlorn hope in such conditions. Someone had pushed a torch into my hand as we launched and I was now sitting at the tiller shining the torch in a sweep. It was choppy and misty with no sign of the ship even. Suddenly I saw something white and set the boat in that direction. I was convinced it was the lifebelt but instead it was the man himself, who, having shed his coat, was trying to keep afloat. We soon had him on the boat, and almost immediately saw the lights of the ship and returned to it. Later I heard the captain telling the man, that it was a chance in a million that he had been rescued on such a night. The man agreed and was grateful. The *Scotia* was only 25 minutes late docking at Holyhead after this incident. Sometime later I was presented with my second Royal Humane Society Testimonial on Vellum for saving life.

Promotion was very slow due to several things, but mainly the depressed state of the economy of the two countries in the period from the mid twenties to the mid thirties. At one stage we were obliged to take a percentage cut in our wages. This bit very hard, as we had young families, mortgages, etc. — yet we were aware of soup kitchens on both sides of the channel. In time, I was made first officer of the *Scotia*, later promoted to captain of the cargo boats, moving up as relief captain of the mail boats.

The Second World War — trooping

When the 1939 war broke out, the crews of the LMS boats refused to man the ships. Yes, they 'refused duties' or 'went on strike', for the simple but valid reason that all the ships, (as were all the LNWR ships before them) were registered in Dublin. The Irish Free State was a neutral country and therefore the crew and their families were not covered in the event of injury or death by enemy action. Someone from London pointed out that they had been registered in Dublin throughout the first war without objection. Mr Parry (Wrench), who had spotted the anomaly and led the protest, replied that Ireland was not neutral during the first war.

Within 48 hours all the ships were re-registered in London and the crews resumed duties, satisfied that they were covered in the event of any enemy action. I should point out of course that all the Free State towns and villages had no blackout regulations, which was very helpful to the enemy ships and planes.

At the beginning of the war RMS *Scotia* was taken over by the Admiralty [as HMT *Scotia*] and sent to Southampton to carry troops to France. She was ideal for this purpose, being fast (25 knots) and manoeuvrable, and many thousands of troops were taken across to Cherbourg, Le Havre, Calais and Dunkirk. Among them were several men from Holyhead and Anglesey who were delighted to talk to us.

The only snag with the *Scotia* as far as the Navy was concerned, was the fact that she was a coal burner, whilst the Navy mostly used oil, which was far more convenient. We had on occasion, to get the crew to help to load tons of coal off a lighter or a coaster, whereas a small tanker could come alongside an oil burner and pump thousands of gallons of fuel oil in a short time with little manual labour.

The *Scotia* had no armaments but relied on her speed and manoeuvrability to get to places. This continued into 1940, with captain, officers and crew getting short periods of leave when relief was available.

This changed radically when the Germans overran Belgium and then the Maginot Line. The advance was so rapid that no one knew exactly where the Germans were at any given time. All ships were now on stand by to evacuate our troops from whichever port was available. I was on leave on 25 May 1940 when a message came to say that I was to return to the *Scotia* immediately as the other captain had been taken ill. I packed my bag and returned to Southampton immediately, where instructions were waiting for us to proceed at once to Dover for further orders.

Dunkirk

On getting to Dover we were told to proceed to Dunkirk and bring back as many troops as possible. The chief engineer had told me that we should re-fuel as we had only around 70 tons. When I put him in the picture about the evacuation, he agreed that there might be over 80 tons, which would be sufficient if we were careful. What we did not know then was that our Admiralty route was not direct to Dunkirk (only a short distance away,) but took us 71 miles into the North Sea.

Off Calais, we were fired upon by German shore batteries, but not hit. Then suddenly the stern was raised out of the water by an explosion. It was obviously a torpedo (later proved to be correct). We checked the hull, but the *Scotia* was not leaking, so we continued towards Dunkirk. As we neared Dunkirk we could see and hear the battle. Constant firing and heavy smoke.

Dunkirk was under a heavy pall of smoke, we could see nothing at all and there were wrecks everywhere. A destroyer came up and asked for our details and when told we were the RMS *Scotia* trooping, they said, 'You are badly wanted over there, take as many as you can'. We proceeded slowly to Dunkirk, past many sunken ships and saw only one enemy plane which dropped its bombs well clear of us. At 9.45 a.m. we got alongside the Mole and loaded well over 3,000 British troops. All were looking spent and exhausted, many were injured and few, if any, carried weapons.

I must refer to the wonderful work done by the embarkation officers. It was an extremely strenuous task and they were doing it with efficiency and dignity, not to mention bravery. I was very impressed with them. I understood that some of them had been working without a break for thirty-six hours.

Having embarked the troops, we left the berth at 3.55 a.m. on Wednesday 29 May. Day was dawning and, as we proceeded easterly along the channel, I saw a troop ship of the tramp type aground, unloading her exhausted passengers into several small craft. We all felt extremely sorry for them but could not help.

To preserve our last lumps of coal, we returned slowly to Dover where we had difficulty mooring, because the engines were almost at a stop and the troops were jam packed on the port side ready to disembark. The reception at Dover was first class, the men being given tea and sandwiches, first aid and, where necessary, clothes. They were then directed to buses or carried to ambulances for hospital treatment. There were volunteers there taking names, numbers, addresses, regiments, etc. before directing them to temporary camps.

My problem was to move the ship, which was now blocking a much-wanted space, but I had no coal, nor was there anyone around to get me some. Eventually I saw a senior naval officer and explained my difficulty to him. He detailed one of his staff to see that I received enough coal to take me to an anchor outside the harbour and then arrange for a full load, so that we could return for more troops.

We were supplied with sufficient coal to take us to Sheerness where we were to re-fuel and take advantage of a short rest. The coal hulk *Agincourt* had very little coal left so we were sent on to Margate Roads and there we found another problem. The *Jolly Days* had coal, but had neither men nor facilities to transfer it. I spoke to the senior naval officer who said he could supply bags and shovels but no labour. I explained the situation to the crew and they all volunteered to transfer the 90 tons of coal from the *Jolly Days* to the *Scotia*. This was very hard and unusual work for most of them, entailing shovelling, loading, holding, hauling or lifting heavy bags. I was extremely proud of them all for doing their utmost to get the *Scotia* ready to return to the hell which was Dunkirk in order to save more lives.

When loading was completed I informed the naval authorities that we were ready and ordered the crew to get as much rest as possible. At 5.45 a.m. instructions came for us to proceed to Dunkirk and we weighed anchor at 7.40 a.m. on Saturday, 1 June and set off following the routes ordered. When about four miles from Dunkirk we were approached by a destroyer which warned us that it was windy off No. 6 buoy. We passed many wrecks as well as boats of all kinds, loaded with exhausted and injured men from the British Expeditionary Force. Shortly after that we were attacked by enemy planes, but our guns kept them away and their bombs fell harmlessly into the sea. Some Spitfires also flew over and were cheered by my crew, but as soon as they disappeared, the German bombers were back with more bombs.

We were now approaching Dunkirk, steering inside the channel buoys to avoid the wrecks, and fully occupied to avoid buoys, bombs and wrecks. I had reduced speed on approaching the entrance but the bombers came again and dropped bombs. One fell only 100ft from our port quarter; another dropped about 50 ft ahead of us. I received orders to proceed to West Mole, to embark French troops and berthed there at 11 a.m. We found Dunkirk fairly quiet except for the occasional round fired by shore batteries.

Immediately on arrival at the West Mole, we started embarking over 2,000 French troops who had been waiting in an orderly fashion for us. As soon as they were aboard, we set off for Sheerness. It was now 12.25 p.m. Again we had to steer carefully because of wrecks, as well as small boats making for Dunkirk. We were clear of No. 6 buoy and travelling at full speed, manoeuvring with the helm, when the bombers returned, sweeping low, firing their guns and dropping bombs. There were at least twelve of them and they followed the same pattern, only this time they hit us with one bomb on the stern and another on the poop deck. The third wave of four bombers came and this time one bomb went straight down the funnel and exploded in the engine room, another fell on the stern.

During all this our guns kept firing at them and their machine-gun bullets were falling on us like hailstones. Mr Seed, the radio officer, had sent an SOS when the first bombs dropped on us, but we were unable to send another because the radio shed had been shattered and the operator thrown out, but he was uninjured. Three of our ten lifeboats had also been smashed. *Scotia* was sinking by the stern and had no engine, so I gave the order to 'Abandon Ship!'.

The French troops could not understand our instructions and were rushing to the boats making it rather difficult as the *Scotia* was keeling over to starboard. Mr Pritchard, the chief officer had to threaten them with his revolver. However, they eventually obeyed my whistle and hand signals and kept clear whilst the boats were being lowered.

Commander Couch of HMS *Esk* (H.15) had received our SOS and came at full speed to our rescue. By now the boat deck on the starboard side was under water, and the vessel was still going over. He, very skilfully, put the bow of his ship close to the forecastle

The HMT Scotia, *sinking off Dunkirk, 1940. HMS* Esk *is alongside.
A mural, taken from this painting, used to be at Euston Station, London.*

head, taking off a large number of troops whilst at the same time his sailors were picking up hundreds out of the sea. Backing his ship out again, he came amid ships on the starboard side, his stern now being against the boat deck, and continued to pick up survivors. The *Scotia* had now rolled over until her forward funnel and mast were in the water. Two more enemy bombers attacked us, dropping four bombs and machine-gunning the poor fellows still swimming in the water or clinging to wreckage.

The *Esk* continued firing and brought down one of the bombers. Commander Couch again skilfully manoeuvred his ship around to the port side, the *Scotia* having gone over until the port bilge keel was out of the water. Hundreds of our soldiers were huddled on the bilge keel. Some of them swam to the *Esk* whilst ropes pulled others up. It was now that we could see the damage caused by the torpedo, which hit us but failed to explode properly on the previous trip. More bombers came over but were driven away by gunfire from HMS *Esk*.

Rescue work continued. Those who were on the bilge were able to climb aboard the destroyer; others swam out and climbed the nets, which incidentally were a boon. By this time, all who were able to help themselves had left the wreck, but there were three who were still there lying seriously injured. One of them was a steward from the *Scotia*; the other two were French soldiers. A rope was thrown from the *Esk*, which I tied around the steward and by means of a boat fall, I was able to help them to ease the jerk as he was lifted aboard. I used the same method with the two French soldiers and , when satisfied that everyone was clear, a boat spar was swung over and I was lifted aboard the *Esk*. We then proceeded to Dover where all were landed.

There were several men who had been picked up by other boats and landed separately at other ports. Eventually I had a complete list of the survivors and regret to say that our final count was 28 of the crew of the *Scotia* missing (another six so seriously injured that they died shortly afterwards). It was also estimated that between 200 and 300 French soldiers were killed or drowned. Many more would have been lost had it not been for the skilful and brave actions of Lieutenant-Commander Couch and the officers and men of the destroyer HMS *Esk*. I have already praised the officers and crew of the *Scotia* in my official report, but have no hesitation at all in repeating my highest praise for their devotion and bravery. I give sincere thanks to all of them.*

To return to Dover and give you some idea of the various things that had to be done. The fit survivors had to be decently clothed, as they had lost everything, they were then put on a train for London

---

* *The Roll of Honour of the crew of HMT* Scotia: *Robert M. Ball; A. W. Bateman; Owen E. Devonald; Edward N. Doughty; John G. Chamberlain; David J. Evans; John H. Hawkins; Hughie Hughes; William Hughes; John Hughes; Thomas P. Hughes; Thomas Higgins; Edwin J. Jones; John P. Jones; William Jones; Richard Jones; Glyn A. Morris; William H. Owen; Idwal Parry; J. Parry; Hugh Pritchard; R. Pritchard; Owen Roberts; Richard H. Roberts; Hugh Roberts; Owen Thomas; R. Thomas; Hugh Williams; John Williams; Edward G. Williams; John H. Williams; Richard J. Williams; Robert Williams; Owen Williams; Thomas Williams.*

where the company superintendent met them and saw them on to the Holyhead train. The company agent took me to Ramsgate where some of my crew had been landed. Some were in hospital, others were sent home on the train. I went to the *Princess Maud*, another of our Holyhead ships, to get some sleep and to await further orders.

The next day, Sunday, 2 June, I travelled to Guildford and visited four hospitals to check on my crew. All of them had been sent there from Dover because of lack of space. I believe that every hospital bed in the south east of England was occupied at that time. From Guildford, I travelled on to London to attend a Court of Enquiry into the loss of the *Scotia*. I arrived too late, but they had re-arranged it for Monday, and I attended that enquiry. Whilst in London, I heard that one of my crew had been picked up on his own and that he firmly believed himself to be the only survivor from the *Scotia*.

After the enquiry I was sent home for a short rest and then joined the *Hibernia* on the Kingstown passenger service. After a few months she was fitted with guns against surface craft and aircraft. I was on leave, but was ordered to return at once as the *Hibernia* had been taken over by the Admiralty for naval service. However, after a couple of weeks, the naval authorities decided that she was not suitable because she was a coal burner. The *Hibernia* returned to the passenger service, retaining the guns and a dozen naval gunners, who remained on the ship until the end of the war.

This is a copy of a letter sent by Lieutenant-Commander Couch, on 12 June 1940, to Captain Harris, Marine Manager, Watford:

> Dear Captain Harris,
> I would like to thank you very much for your letter and to say how much it was appreciated.
> I think you would like to know that I made a special report on the magnificent work done by Captain W. H. Hughes on the occasion. With the ship on fire and sinking, in fact beyond all hope, his only

thought was of rescuing the wounded, which he did with great energy, and no regard for his own safety.

It was with some difficulty that I persuaded him to leave the ship after all the rescue work had been completed.

With many thanks,

Yours sincerely

(Signed) Richard Couch. (Lieut. Commander)

Three months later the destroyer *Esk* struck a mine. Commander Couch and all but one of his crew were lost.

From Captain J. D. Harris, Marine Manager, Watford to Captain W .H. Hughes:

Dear Captain Hughes,

I received yesterday a very nice letter from young Roberts, my ex Booth Line Cadet, who was your Pilot on the *SCOTIA* at the time of the sinking. The latter part of Roberts' letter is a splendid testimony of your good self, and I feel I should give it to you word for word. It is as follows:

The example set by Captain Hughes to all those aboard the *SCOTIA* was grand. He upheld the highest traditions of our Merchant Navy, when the persuasive calling of the *Esk's* Commander went unheard until he saw that every man had left the ship and had a fair chance of survival. Decorations have been awarded for less brave deeds. I feel honoured to have served such a man.

It is signed by Captain J. D. Harris, Marine Manager, LMS *Watford*.

Early in 1941 I attended an investiture at Buckingham Palace and was awarded the Distinguished Service Cross by His Majesty King George VI for 'outstanding bravery' at Dunkirk. Several members of my crew were also given awards for bravery.

The decorations and medals of Captain William Hughes.
L–R: Distinguished Service Cross; British War Medal, 1914-20; Mercantile Marine
Medal, 191418; 1939–45 Star; Atlantic Star, 1939–45; 1939–45 War Medal.
Bottom: Dunkerque Medal, 1940 (France).

Back to Holyhead

On this Irish Sea service, enemy aircraft and the occasional submarine were constantly attacking our ships. Our sister ship, the *Cambria*, gave a good account of herself with her guns when she was attacked by a German bomber with an aerial torpedo and machine-guns. The torpedo missed the ship but machine-gun fire killed Mr Jones, the third officer. This area was fairly free from submarines until later in the war, when a few ships were sunk and many others damaged.

At the end of the war we had two passenger ships, the *Cambria* and the *Hibernia*, with the *Princess Maud* as stand-by ship. The *Maud*, as she was affectionately called, had a wonderful record of war service. Originally on the Larne–Stranraer route she was transferred to Holyhead. As the *Cambria* and *Hibernia* were getting old (1920) and wartime had prevented them getting serviced as they were used to, the company decided to order two new ships to take over the route, with *Princess Maud* as the third ship. This was to be the future pattern. The new ships were to be 5,200 tons and named *Cambria* and *Hibernia* and were to be built by Harland & Wolff at Belfast.

We had several ex-servicemen joining the ships as officers and crew and I recall one funny incident concerning an ex-naval man. I had gone to my cabin to sign the papers, ready for the customs officer at Holyhead, when I realised that the speaking tube from the bridge had been left open. I was just about to tell them to switch it off, when I heard an ex-naval officer asking, 'For how long do you think we will have to carry the old dinosaurs?' Obviously referring to myself, my brother Jesse, and Captain Marsh!

A few weeks later we were in thick fog off the Stack when I was called to the bridge by the same naval officer. When I reached there, he said he would prefer me to take the ship into the harbour because of the fog and as he was inexperienced. I took over and brought her safely to the mooring. As I handed her back to him I couldn't help saying 'Thankfully there are still things for the 'Old Dinosaurs' to do.' He

Captain William Hughes showing Lady Maud Montgomery (mother of the field marshal) around the bridge of the Hibernia *during a wartime crossing to Ireland.*

85

The MV Cambria *berthed at Holyhead.*

looked guilty but made no comment.

I remained in command of the *Hibernia* until May 1949 when I took over command of the new MV *Cambria,* 5,200tons; the largest cross-channel ferry at the time, and luxuriously fitted throughout. Her sister ship the *Hibernia,* had arrived a month ahead of her. Both ships were built in Harland & Wolff, Belfast, for British Transport Commission, our owners since January 1948. The ships were like an hotel, with carpets and wide stairs and ample room for 2,000 passengers to sit or sleep. The accommodation was in two classes, with saloons and promenade facilities for day crossings and deluxe double berth state rooms for 1st Class passengers and six berth cabins for 2nd Class travellers.

They were quite manoeuvrable, in spite of their size, and proved to be excellent sea boats, but with a tendency to roll in certain currents. This was cured later when they were both fitted with Denny Brown stabilizers. I took the *Cambria* out on her maiden crossing in May 1948 and it was quite an event. My thoughts went back to the first *Cambria,* the *Arvon,* the *Miss Pritchard,* the *Beeswing* and the *Deccan* and to my father emerging from under that huge sea in Morocco. Quite a change had taken place in ships during my lifetime.

The pattern now was to have one night sailing in winter, and twice daily in summer, with the *Princess Maud* on stand-by. There were still shortages of certain items in Britain. Certain food was almost impossible to buy, clothes rationing remained and as a result there were many who took advantage of the double sailing to travel on the early trip to Dublin in the luxurious surroundings, spend the day shopping for food and materials and return on the late sailing, hoping that the customs officers would be busy with someone else.

On 30 March, the old *Hibernia* (1920) was towed to Barrow for demolition and on 17 May of the same year the *Cambria* (1920) went to the same fate at Milford Haven. Both ships had given excellent service in war and peace and were very handsome vessels. They were ideal for the service at Holyhead.

In August 1950, after 52 years at sea, I retired, hopefully to live a life of continued good health and leisure.

Facing: Holyhead Maritime Museum, 29 July 1986. Front row: Capt. W. E. Williams; Capt. W. H. Hughes, DSC; Capt. Peters; Capt. Griffiths. Middle row: Capt. I. Pritchard; Capt. Thomas; Capt. Milburn; Capt. Rowlands; Capt. Enrys Williams; Capt. Owyn Jones; Capt. Howells; Capt. L. Evans; Capt. Butterworth; Capt. Hubert Hughes. Back row: Capt. Ted Jones; Capt. Raymond Jones; Capt. Merrick; Capt. Parri Hughes; Capt. Ted Morris; Capt. Powell; Capt. Crane; Capt. Mason; Capt. Walter Williams; Capt. Alex Robertson.

S.S. Retirement

Captain William Henry Hughes, DSC, retired as commodore of the British Transport Ships at Holyhead. He thoroughly enjoyed 'SS Retirement,' although he suffered many tragedies, especially the loss of his only son Wynn Hope Hughes, in October 1953 aged 33, and his grandson Lewis in 1985, aged 21, a student at Edinburgh University. Both died of cancer,

His wife Barbara died in 1972. Originally from Tanygrisiau, her family had also moved to Liverpool where she had taught at an infants school. They were married in David Street Chapel, Liverpool, in 1916 and moved to Holyhead in 1918, where they spent the rest of their days. They were blessed with four children Wynn, Elinor, Barbara and Menna. Elinor became my wife and we had three children, Eleri, Hefin and Luned. Menna married Alun Edwards and they had two children Jennifer and Lewis.

Captain Hughes loved children, and thoroughly enjoyed taking them out in the pram. Later he taught them how to row and sail, and had infinite patience with them.

His daughter Barbara looked after him very carefully from 1972 until his death, although she was a full time secondary school teacher.

When he retired, Captain Hughes received a first class railway pass from the company, entitling him to travel anywhere in the country. This he made full use of, travelling regularly to various places, particularly between Holyhead and Liverpool. Why Liverpool? You will recall that his family moved there when trade declined in Porthmadog. Many of his extended family still lived in the city and he was given a great welcome on each visit by Mary Edwards, his older sister and her family, Oswald and family, (yes the same Oswald who went missing in Australia!) and Edith, the spinster.

Captain Arthur, who suffered greatly as a result of his war wounds, died in 1955. Captain Hughes called regularly to see

Captain William Hughes with his daughters: Eleanor, Menna and Barbara.

Arthur's wife and his two daughters and, of course, he visited his youngest sister Jennie Jones who later moved to Rhosneigr to live.

The family and their husbands, wives and offspring took an active part in the civic and religious life of the city of Liverpool.

During these train journeys he would strike a conversation with all kinds of interesting people and regale us with tales of whom he had met. He also enjoyed visiting bookshops and usually had a book in his pocket, mostly to do with religion or psychology or some maritime activity. As his shelves were already full, he would often call at our house on his way home and ask Elinor to keep the book until he had made room for it!

Captain Hughes never learnt to drive, and used to walk everywhere, but he thoroughly enjoyed being a passenger in his daughter Barbara's car. There were regular trips to Chester, Liverpool and of course Borth-y-gest. It was Barbara who looked after him following the death of his wife Barbara in 1972.

On the 29 July 1986, just before his 100th birthday, Captain Hughes was invited to attend a special gathering at the Holyhead Maritime Museum at St Elbod's Church. Among those assembled were 28 master mariners as well as senior members of the local and county councils and officials. Also present were the Duke of Westminster, Aled Eames (the noted maritime historian) and Bryn Parry (the county archivist.)

The first paragraph of the editorial in *Maritime Wales*, No. 10, reads as follows:

> This is the tenth number of *Maritime Wales*, published in the year in which one of the great grand masters of the sea, Captain William Henry Hughes, D.S.C. originally from Borthygest and now of Holyhead, approaches his hundredth birthday. This volume includes as a major feature, a tribute to him from the editors and we are sure that his many friends in the maritime world will wish to be associated with us in expressing our gratitude for all he has taught us of a past which he alone can recall.

Aled Eames was fulsome in his praise for the help he had received from Captain Hughes, and went as far as to say that Captain Hughes had inspired him to write his maritime books. He particularly stressed his excellent memory and unerring accuracy, even describing one particular event when he had phoned him late one evening and had been given more than he expected in answer. As a result Aled decided to check the facts only to find that they were correct in every detail.

Several others spoke including Captain/County Councillor Alex Robertson and Captain Idwal Pritchard, son of the first officer on the *Scotia*.

A photograph was taken of the master mariners present. On his 100th birthday, 24 August 1986, Captain Hughes and his family were invited to a special reception aboard RMS *St Columba* at the station in Holyhead. Captain Leonard Evans (the Commodore) presented him with a painting 'The Edward Seymour', the ship owned jointly by his father and grandfather, in which his father had made such a name for himself. The painting was by Captain

Captain Hughes unveiling the memorial plaque on the railway platform at Holyhead to the officers, crew and soldiers who died when the SS Scotia was sunk at Dunkirk in 1940.

Sandy Balfour, a noted local maritime artist.

In the early hours of 15 January 1987, Captain William Henry Hughes died peacefully after a short illness, aged 100 years and 5 months, after a full and well-lived life. He is buried with his wife Barbara and son Wynn Hope in Maeshyfryd Cemetery, Holyhead.

The gravestone of Captain Hughes in Maeshyfryd Cemetery, Holyhead.

Glossary

William Alexander Madocks — MP for Boston, Lincolnshire, the second son of a King's Counsel, who happened to visit the area on holiday, fell for the beauty of it, but, more importantly, recognised the potential and acted upon it. The area owes him a great debt.

spar — a thick pole on the mast of a sailing ship to extend the sails.
bar — bank of sand at the mouth of a river
hove-to — anchored
more chain — more anchor chain to compensate for the tide.
spellabout — taking turns.
tacking — setting sail to slant to the wind.
topsail — square sail carried on yard set on to topmast.
staysail — see sketch of 'Beeswing' sails.
windlass — a simple winch to crank up heavy weights.
turnabout — taking turns.
Skaw — a shipping lane off Denmark.
Q-ship — an armed ship disguised as a merchant ship.
A/B — Able Seaman.
O/S — Ordinary Seaman.
B. E. F. — British Expeditionary Force.
Alfred Holt — famous shipowner.
Cunard — a famous shipping company.
sheets — ropes fastened to a sail.
poop deck — the high deck at the stern of a ship.
furling — rolling up a sail.
Doldrums — a region of light winds and calms near the Equator.
bowsprit — a bar projecting from the bow of a ship.
scuppers — holes in the side of a ship, level with the deck, to allow
    water to exit.
sheering — going off course.
tiller — lever to move the rudder of a boat.
port quarter — left side of a ship.

starboard quarter — right side of a ship.

Obligatory daily provisions 1904 (per person)

1lb bread
3 quarts water
$1^1/_4$lb beef
$1^1/_4$ lb pork (including bacon)
$^1/_2$ lb flour
$^1/_3$ pt peas
$^1/_8$ oz tea
$^1/_2$ oz coffee
2oz sugar

Acknowledgements and Bibliography

My grateful thanks are due to:

The staff of Gwynedd Archives at Caernarfon and to the late Bryn Parry (County Archivist) who knew about the recordings and urged me to publish them; Mr Ivor Wynne Jones (journalist/author) for the copy of 'The Irish Lights Papers' confirming Captain Hughes' story of the event; Mr Len Jones, Holyhead, for transferring the original details from large spools to cassettes, thus facilitating my work; my sisters-in-law, Barbara Hughes and Menna Edwards, for checking the final draft and for providing photographs; my sister, Enid Francis, for typing the original copy of the book and spending hours in the archives in Caernarfon; my brother, Owen, and my son, Hefin, and daughters, Eleri Hunter and Luned Francis, for reading the proofs and helping me to understand a little about these marvellous computers; Mr Arthur John Edwards, Liverpool for details of the family; Mr Alister Williams of Bridge Books.

Finally, without naming them, my thanks to all who have helped or encouraged me with the book.

Dewi Francis, Holyhead, 2006.

W. A. Madocks and the Wonder of Wales, Elizabeth Beasley.
Ships and Seamen of Anglesey, Aled Eames.
Porthmadog Ships, Emrys Hughes and Aled Eames.
Gold, Frankenstein and Manure, Ivor Wynne Jones.
Porthmadog, Llanw Ddoe, Myfanwy Morris.
The Battle with the Horn, Alan Villiers.
Packet to Ireland, M. Elis-Williams,
The Holyhead Steamers of the LNWR, Pearsall & Davies
Holyhead, the Story of a Port, D. Lloyd Hughes and Dorothy M. Williams